Learning the Fiddler's Ways

Learning the Fiddler's Ways

Matthew G. Guntharp

Foreword by Samuel P. Bayard

Introduction by Robert C. Doyle

Keystone Books

The Pennsylvania State University Press

University Park and London

For Cindy

Frontispiece, map, and diagrams by Chris van Dyck

Music autography by Hugh Johnson

Library of Congress Cataloging in Publication Data

Guntharp, Matthew G
Learning the fiddler's ways.
(Keystone books)
1. Fiddle tunes—History and criticism. I. Title.
ML3561.F5G8 787'.1'0714 79-65825
ISBN 0-271-00237-9 cloth
ISBN 0-271-02248-4 paper

Contents

List of Fingering Diagrams

List of Tunes

To the Reader

This book is written for everyone who wants to know more about fiddling and fiddle tunes—both oldtime and bluegrass—and would like to meet some of the delightful people that keep an old folk art very much alive.

The message here from my partner Bob Doyle and me is that in many ways you too can get fun out of fiddling. Some of you will follow us and learn to fiddle or, if you're already a fiddler, maybe learn to play better. You'll certainly learn to listen more keenly—whether as a square dancer, a caller, or an enjoyer—if you catch the enthusiasm of fiddlers like the ones we write about. You can learn the rewards of collecting fiddle tunes, ranging from classroom or vacation projects to lifelong hobbies to careers in folklore, as well as some of the pitfalls we narrowly missed as beginning collectors. Best of all, you can learn how to meet some dedicated and colorful folk artists, as we did by seeking out nearby places, where, perhaps to your surprise, fiddling still thrives.

A little biography will help you to understand what this book is and what it isn't. Bob Doyle and I wanted to learn to fiddle, partly for fun and partly to build a repertoire for a band we were forming. Our desire to learn fiddling led us into the Buffalo Valley, a central Pennsylvania farm region where the fiddler's art is held in high esteem.

In our quest we soon found that the fiddler's art is bound up with his tunes—and with his personality. Every tune and tune version reflects a fiddler's musical background, skill, and taste. In this way a fiddler's playing affects a tune's character. This discovery led us into collecting tunes both as entities unto themselves and also as reflections of fiddlers' stylistic and individual influences and preferences. We felt, as well, that the stories and lore the fiddlers told about playing their tunes are very much a part of the fiddler's art. Since we live near Penn State University, we consulted an eminent folklorist there, Samuel P. Bayard, about proper collection procedures. We also took some helpful courses at Penn State. Our studies led both to the acceptance of our Buffalo Valley tapes by the University Library and the Library of Congress, and to the establishment of a fiddlers' competition at the Central Pennsylvania Festival of the Arts (where a growing number of women participants have been welcomed into this historically male preserve).

Bob Doyle gives more details in his Introduction about our entry into the fiddlers' world. My purpose here is simply to emphasize that this is a *learning* book, designed to help you learn what we have learned. Although our project is endorsed by folklorists of Samuel Bayard's stature, we make no claim to high scholarship; this is no revelation of hitherto lost folk material or of new refinements in folkloristic methodology. Our intention is more modest and widely directed: a celebration of the joy of learning the fiddler's ways.

Preface

To all the fiddlers and their families who helped Bob Doyle and me in our project, I offer my sincerest appreciation. Without their cooperation and time there would, quite simply, be no collection and no book. I gained more from them than I will ever be able to repay. Through this book, I hope their music will reach beyond the relatively few who are now able to enjoy it.

Bob and I tried to build personal relationships with the fiddlers we met. Personal interaction offers the most to all in the study of folk art. In view of our collecting approach, and in order to relate our experiences accurately, I felt it essential that this book be written from a personal viewpoint.

Much of *Learning the Fiddler's Ways* consists of dialogues transcribed from interview tapes. These dialogues serve several important functions. First, they portray our fiddler friends in a way no descriptions can. Second, they demonstrate how we elicited information from players without seeming excessively academic. Third, couched in what sometimes appears to be just rambling conversation are often very important musicological points. One must learn to recognize and focus attention on such points. Finally, dialogue demonstrates the level of conscious understanding that the fiddlers have of their art, as well as their ability or inability to articulate it.

Learning the Fiddler's Ways could never have become a reality without the help of many people. Samuel Bayard's help was fundamental. For his guidance I shall always be grateful. Stanley Weintraub, director of Penn State's Institute for the Arts and Humanistic Studies, assisted us in the acquisition and administration of funding for our project and reviewed the manuscript for this book. His help leaves me deeply in his debt. I offer my sincerest gratitude to Carol Ballew, Judy Hewes, and Hugh Johnson for their help in preparing the manuscript. I would like to thank Glenn Ruby and John Pickering of the Penn State Press—Glenn for his thoughtful editorial suggestions and Jack for his help in defining and expressing some of the goals of the book. I especially want to take this opportunity to thank my colleague, Bob Doyle, for his extensive contributions. His work in the field was invaluable. Its importance to my work will be apparent throughout the book. Also, without his prodding and support I might never have completed *Learning the Fiddler's Ways*. Finally, I wish to thank all those others who in any way helped with the project. I would like to thank The Pennsylvania State University and the Pennsylvania Council on the Arts for their financial assistance. Because of all this support, some of Pennsylvania's fiddling will never die.

Foreword

Samuel P. Bayard

As a Pennsylvania folk-music collector whose active work had ceased, I used to believe that changing times had destroyed the chances of much additional collecting, and that instrumental folk music, like folk songs, was largely "on the way out." As I saw the picture in 1963, there were indeed symptoms of a decline, with community fifers well-nigh gone, and fiddlers locally scarcer. But I had yet to learn that the condition was only temporary. In this book, Matthew Guntharp and Bob Doyle have taught me the lesson that, although circumstances have sometimes altered the way tunes are learned and spread abroad, the practice of genuine traditional fiddling is by no means fading away. In fact, in Pennsylvania it seems to be experiencing something very much like a "comeback," with higher technical standards than those of former times, and numerous upcoming young players appearing in towns as well as in the countryside. The whole picture is very different from that of thirty years ago, when some "oldtime" fiddlers were feeling rejected, while many young folks were referring to their music as "that awful corn."

These younger players' backgrounds may differ, but not their objectives, which extend from finding personal satisfaction, to square-dance fiddling, to professional entertaining. The aim that seems to unite them all, however, is that of preserving traditional playing styles and favorite tunes, both old and new. Actually, this is the same progression followed by the authors of this book—with whom an exhilarating adventure in learning and enjoying became supplemented by a serious effort to gather up and save the traditional music which these musicians were actively playing. The authors' experiences, in short, taught them so much that their book became something more than an interesting narrative about their musician friends and teachers, and developed into a sort of guide for other amateur collectors who might want a share in the work of saving this art and this music.

For instance, among many perceptive observations coming out of their meetings with the traditional players, the authors give us some counsel about how to cope with—and turn to benefit—the disappointments and frustrations that inevitably form part of this kind of "rescue work." (What collector has not heard chilling words like "haven't picked up the fiddle for years" . . . "couldn't raise a tone" . . . "forgot the most of my tunes," etc., etc.?) Also, their remarks about what to do when interviewing the players—attitudes to take, items to watch for and inquire about, matters that should be brought up in conversation—are bound to be helpful to anyone wanting to learn and save these tunes. The same is true of their advice concerning the use of tape recorders in collecting, so as to assure good, transcribable records of the music, apart from the instrumental accompaniments. The diagrams that show the common fiddling keys, with all their overlapping, are features that one seldom sees in books of this sort; and I know by experience that they not only help one in learning to play "oldtime," but are extremely informative about the structure, the melodic turns, and the whole idiom of the tunes themselves. And the observations about how youngsters learn tunes and pick up the technique of playing are something I have not seen discussed in detail in any description of the country fiddler's art.

On the whole, I am very glad that Matthew and Bob have chosen to write this book, and I am also hopeful that it will result in the rescue and further enjoyment of many more of our old instrumental folk melodies.

Introduction

Robert C. Doyle

Next to the human voice, the fiddle is the most popular folk instrument in North America. *Learning the Fiddler's Ways* is a story about the fiddlers Matthew Guntharp and I met in Central Pennsylvania, specifically the Buffalo Valley of Union and Snyder counties. Some of those we met play frequently; some had not played in years. But one characteristic all possess is a love of their music and a willingness to share it.

Having taken an interest in fiddling, our search for fiddlers living in the Buffalo Valley began when Matthew and I decided that we needed to find players to teach us to play square dance tunes. Our subsequent collecting took its first step forward on September 15, 1973, when I asked Dick Nellis, an instructor of economics at the Williamsport Area Community College and a resident of Penns Creek, "Who plays the fiddle around here?" His answer was "Old Joe Bell, I think!" No one in town seemed to know whether Joe Bell played any more, so we decided to find out.

Since Gary Bell, Joe Bell's grandnephew, was within earshot when I spoke with Dick Nellis, Joe Bell knew I was coming well before I knocked on his door. The fiddle was on his sofa, and he was rosining his bow. Gary told his Uncle Joe that some strangers were asking around about fiddlers, and that he ought to expect a visit. I'm sure that Joe's initial curiosity about us matched ours about him.

Joe Dietrich, then a member of our band, Bob Doyle and the Buffalo Chipkickers, was with me on that first visit. He was as eager as Matthew and I to learn old fiddle tunes.

Accepting our seemingly strange visit and unusual requests, Joe Bell struggled through "Just Because." With a nod he explained, "That's an oldie; you ought to remember that!" I smiled and returned the nod, embarrassed that I never heard the tune before. Later in the visit I discarded my embarrassment in favor of curiosity and persistence.

I met Joe Bell in 1973 when he was 71 years old. He was a retired woodworker and a member of the Penns Creek Volunteer Fire Company. He lived with his wife Anne in a small house at the lower end of town. Joe learned to play the fiddle from his father, Henry E. Bell, who had performed in the region through his adult life. He closed his career around 1936 when his last band, The Jacks Mountain Stubble Jumpers, broke up.

Around town Joe Bell is well respected and admired not only for his once-superb fiddling but more for his positive and pleasing personality. It surprised me that at times he had qualms about playing for strangers.

Joe Bell usually played only phrases of tunes for us. This seemed strange, but after later conversations with Harry Daddario (see Chapter 5), we found we were not alone with the problem. Harry is a fiddler, and he and Joe have known each other for years. Harry told us that Joe Bell would never play a whole tune even for him. Harry commented that Joe Bell used to play "all them ragtime tunes," and he assured us that Joe Bell could once play the old-fashioned square dance tunes as well as anyone in the valley. During our interview and much to my beginner's frustration, Joe could not be prodded into playing them.

I approached Joe Bell with hopes that he would play a hearty repertoire of square dance music. I can hardly express the disappointment I felt when he insisted on playing only short phrases. I could barely restrain myself from saying, "Damn it, Mr. Bell, will you please play your fiddle!" My patience paid a substantial dividend though, because he poured forth many a story about dances he had played long ago. If Harry Daddario, his longtime friend, could not persuade him to play, what chance did we as total strangers have? Instead, I learned to appreciate Joe Bell from another point of view. Instead of recording tunes, we recorded stories. Here are excerpts from our first interview with Joe:

Bob: How about the "Bummer's Reel"?

Joe Bell: Well, now that's just it. That's three flats and two flats. [He played a phrase of "Bummer's Reel."] Now this other guy, he played it somewhere. Now, wait a minute. I don't play it that way. I don't go to G. I don't play it in the key he played it in.

Bob: Well, that's OK. You play it the way you play it.

Joe Bell: Yeah, the "Bummer's Reel," I wrote it down, and he [the name slipped his memory] played in G, and I play it in E and B flat. [Harry Daddario played "Bummer's Reel" in G.]

I was puzzled at why Joe played in flat keys. From my experiences with country fiddling I took it for granted that most fiddlers played in the sharp keys of G, D, A, and C. Either I was mistaken, or Joe Bell had developed some highly unusual habits. I probed further, this time asking about "Durang's Hornpipe":

Joe Bell: "Durang's Hornpipe!"
Bob: In E flat?
Joe Bell: That is, I play it in E flat. I need some rosin; I need some of everything. Yeah, it's wrote in D, and I play it in E flat.
Bob: Is it easier to play in E flat?
Joe Bell: Oh, I believe it is for me.
Joe Dietrich: You have a lot of those tunes in flats, don't you?
Joe Bell: Oh, I play everything, a lot of C flat and E flat.
Bob: Why?
Joe Bell: It's so much easier to finger. I mean it's not such a scratchy tone, you know. Anything a sharp key, you know, G, A, and C, yeah, they're sharps, and you have open strings, see!
Bob: Do most fiddlers play in flats rather than sharps? How about "Brennan's Reel"?
Joe Bell: I can get over 'em if I can think of 'em.

It turned out that Joe Bell had learned to read music, but only after he had already learned enough traditional tunes to play for square dances. From sheet music he learned the popular tunes of his day, and he began to transpose his repertoire of square dance tunes into flat keys. This accounts for his difficulties in trying to play the old-fashioned tunes we wanted to hear. Playing in E flat and B flat, for example, requires the techniques usually beyond all but highly skilled players. Playing in sharp keys allows a player the advantage of using his open strings. Sharp keys are consequently easier for oldtime fiddlers.

I began this project thinking that reading music was taboo for the true country or folk fiddler. On that account I thought Joe Bell was a disappointment. In time I discovered that learning to read music was not necessarily a detriment, and I soon corrected my misguided prejudice. From written music a fiddler may indeed learn tunes, but his bowing technique, rhythms, and ornamentations are invariably learned through the folk process of imitation and experimentation. From Joe Bell I learned that it does not matter whether a fiddler reads music; the important thing is the nature of his playing.

After I exhausted every means of prodding Joe Bell into playing tunes, I turned to his stories. He was absolutely delighted about this request and proceeded with an animation that kept us laughing all afternoon. It began when he asked me where I lived. "State College," I replied. "Oh yeah," he said. "I remember the time we played up there. I'll tell you all about it." In Joe Bell's estimation this was indeed the square dance of a lifetime.

Joe Bell: We played up there at State College. Yeah, we played down at the [American] Legion, you know, in the basement, and there I run into the best square dance caller I ever seen in my life, this Jack Stover from Millheim and Doc Stover. Jack was the banjo player [tenor banjo], and he got us the job up there. He said, "Don't worry about the caller; they have their own." I said, "That suits me fine!" We went up there and went in. We were getting ready, then a guy came over. I don't know who, maybe the commander or something. He asked who the boss was. They said the fiddle player. "Now I want to tell you something," he said. "This is a square dance; you play no round dance!" Now, believe you me, they ran us so damn ragged that night, oh boy! We never went back! The guys, we were used to, the guitar, you know, their fingers were tough! Christ! You could take and ooze the blood out of their fingers. I just changed tunes and didn't take the fiddle from under my chin. They just stood ready and they [the dancers] moved right in. This guy, he didn't say, "Play this or that." He said, "You play, and I'll call." Whatever we started in on he had something to call. And when we was done at the end of it, he was done calling. I said I ain't never seen a guy like that; he was the best caller I ever run into.

Joe Dietrich: Well didn't the people dancing get tired?

Joe Bell: Oh, they was crazy, they was! There was a set on the floor, you know. They had ten sets at one time, and all the other sets stood ready. As soon as they was done, they moved off, and the other ones moved right in. We just changed tunes, and I didn't take the fiddle from under my chin! He [the caller] came over to us when we were done and said, "I gotta congratulate you; I didn't hear you repeat one number all night, not one number!" And I tell you he didn't repeat one call!

Joe Dietrich: How long did you play?

Joe Bell: From eight to ten, and then they gave us ten minutes, and they hollered for more. Then we went from ten to twelve. Then they wanted us back! The guys said, "You son-of-a-bitch, you play it yourself!" Oh no, they never would play there no more. "Jigger" Bateman was the saxophone player, and when we were setting up, the steam pipes were pretty close. We were just in hot water. We told the guy [Legion Commander], "Can't you turn that damn stuff off? These guys [dancers] are killing us on the floor, and you are roasting us here." They went and shut off the steam. That settled that!

In his seventies, Joe Bell is badly out of practice. The tunes he had played on his fiddle long ago have deteriorated into short phrases. The picture he painted that day of his early adventures certainly was vivid. It captured the humor and genuine admiration he had for those who shared his art: players, callers, and dancers. My immediate reaction to him, I suppose, was typical of a novice collector during his first interview. I was eager to collect tunes. When he refused to play entire pieces I thought he was being stubborn, but in time I accepted his explanation, "I just can't get over 'em no more." I had to search further for players who would and could play the square dance tunes we wanted to learn.

From this very important first attempt I learned several lessons about collecting. Not every player in the valley, or anywhere else for that matter, is current or practiced on his instrument. Rather than being a condemnation of one's ability, being "rusty" is more an indication that the affairs of life, the withering of age, and the redirection of personal interests have taken a toll of the fiddler's skill.

Joe Bell played an important role in our collecting project in the Buffalo Valley. He was not only the first fiddler we met, but he referred us to other players, notably Harry Daddario. "Old Harry will play a few tunes for ya," he chuckled. The meeting with Joe Bell helped me work on my interviewing techniques and prepared me for the upcoming situations where fiddlers were more practiced and willing to play. In this way Joe Bell proved to be a good beginning.

Initially we planned to restrict our collecting effort to the New Berlin-Penns Creek area. As we discovered players throughout the region, we extended our reach to include the entire Buffalo Valley. Harry Daddario of New Berlin, the first active fiddler we found, became the focal point around which our project spiraled. Eventually we included fiddlers from well beyond that small town: David Bell of Lewisburg RD 3; Ralph Sauers of Dice; Marvin Kratzer of Winfield; Joe Bell of Penns Creek; Archie Miller of Lewisburg RD 3; Elmer Shaffer of Millheim; and Bob

Cheeseman, formerly of Bellefonte, Pennsylvania.

Our field trips became more frequent and more intense as we found more fiddlers. The end of each trip always provided an opportunity to return to my parents' home along Penns Creek for a good meal and some much-needed rest. In addition to providing a relaxing atmospere, my parents, Ed and Arvella Doyle, often assisted us in locating fiddle players. There were moments during our first visits to fiddlers' homes when it was very helpful to be the son of someone living in the area.

The Buffalo Valley is no stranger to me. It lies approximately fifty miles east of State College, Pennsylvania, the home of The Pennsylvania State University. As a boy, I had spent summers traveling through the back roads near New Berlin and learned the basic layout of the valley. From my travels I became acquainted with the people of the valley, but I never realized when I was a boy that I would later be searching for the people about whom this book is written—fiddlers.

Immediately upon returning from our fiddler-seeking trips to Penns Creek and the Buffalo Valley, I took the interview tapes to Professor Samuel P. Bayard of Penn State, who constructively criticized our efforts. He sent me back, despite the mistakes, for futher interviews. He seemed certain that if we were persistent, we would learn and perhaps collect a great deal. Sam's encouragement came at a very good time.

In 1944, Sam Bayard stated in *Hill Country Tunes* that there was little sustained effort at collecting the vast amount of instrumental folk music in America. This argument in many ways still holds, but times are changing. Collecting efforts made by both professional and amateur collectors are expanding, as evidenced by the growing archives of American instrumental folk music at several universities throughout the country. Professor Bayard has ceased his active collecting and is cataloging and annotating his vast collection for publication.

Our relationship with Professor Samuel P. Bayard was close and continual. With him we discussed every aspect of our work. He served as our mentor when we returned from collecting. He never visited fiddlers with us; that was our job exclusively. He patiently sat through every field recording from beginning to end. We gained direction and confidence from Sam Bayard, enough to manage a large undertaking. In addition to these contributions, he served as an Honorary Judge at the Central Pennsylvania Festival of the Arts Fiddlers' Competition, July 1975, 1976, 1977, and 1978.

Our project's funding and administrative support came primarily from Professor

Stanley Weintraub, Director of the Institute for Arts and Humanistic Studies at the University Park Campus of The Pennsylvania State University. He directed me to inquire for direct support from the Penn State Office of Gifts and Endowments. I did, and we were fortunate to receive a grant for our work. Further, we received help from the Pennsylvania Council on the Arts in Harrisburg. Managing these two grants would have been impossible had it not been for the advice and guidance of Professor Weintraub. In addition to grant management, Stan Weintraub offered administrative and substantive assistance in the preparation of the collection in general. Like Professor Bayard, Professor Weintraub was part of the project almost from the beginning.

Matthew and I knew well that we could not possibly reach all the fiddlers we hoped to reach by going from one to another as we had done in the earlier stages of our project. We had to devise a means whereby we could provide some sort of event which would attract fiddlers. What could be better than to have a fiddlers' competition?

Each summer, in July, State College hosts one of the largest arts festivals in the Commonwealth. We considered the Central Pennsylvania Festival of the Arts an ideal setting for a fiddlers' competition. After a short meeting on a cold December evening, the planning committee of the Central Pennsylvania Festival of the Arts agreed to sponsor the competition.

The competition was a tremendous success. We found that in addition to providing excellent entertainment for a very enthusiastic and receptive audience, we created a forum for active fiddlers, many of whom we hoped to interview later. Our first competition in 1975 drew fiddlers from several nearby counties. Competitions in later years have drawn players from throughout the state—evidence of the growing popularity and success we have enjoyed.

Fiddling is a folk art. It is not a fine art cultivated under society's watchful eye. Terms like "by ear," "picked it up," and "licks" are typical of the easy and flowing nature of fiddling. We rarely heard a fiddler use the term "violin" except when he was particularly pleased with his instrument. Harry Daddario would say, "Now Bob, this here is a good violin," but without exception the favorite instrument is a fiddle.

The fiddle players we met and their families are keeping alive a folk art. Their music is passed from one generation to the next, molded by the gradual and ever-changing tastes of the listeners and players. Styles and techniques provide a continuity within fiddling and at the same time allow change.

In each interview session my job was to keep the questions flowing: who, what, when, where, and how. Matthew increasingly accompanied me on the trips, especially if he had the opportunity to play along with David Bell or Harry Daddario because more and more Matthew became fascinated with the learning process and certain technical aspects of fiddling styles. While he and the fiddlers were swapping tunes, I played the guitar accompaniment, or "backtime." During the course of events I learned to play the fiddle myself. I had to. I found the fiddle more challenging than any other instrument I ever attempted. It seems to defy mastery except by the very few who make it their life's avocation, and for some their life's work.

Learning the Fiddler's Ways describes our quest. Surely, you will notice our occasional disappointments, frustrations, and mistakes. Sam Bayard told us that we were gaining valuable experience—and he was right. In learning how to collect folk music, as either an amateur or a professional, mistakes are unavoidable, but they can be remedied. As musicians, we found it easy to maintain an interest in fiddling, but in order to accomplish a little more we followed and accepted Sam Bayard's advice.

Events which at first set a working pace slowly became standard procedure. I attempted to find out as much as possible about a fiddler before knocking on his door. The first visit to a fiddler's home normally followed an introductory telephone call. I always asked when it would be convenient for me to stop by, and I made doubly sure I arrived on time.

At first, interviews were difficult and time-consuming, with conversations meandering from topic to topic. I often felt that both the fiddlers and their families were "feeling me out." And in the beginning I think I tended to talk too much. I took too active a role when I should have been listening. Sam Bayard pointed this out to me when we listened to the first interview tapes in his office. Eventually, I learned to allow the fiddlers to move at their own pace while I simply tried to guide the overall direction. I learned the value of silence and well-directed questioning. Learning to be quiet was a chore; I wanted too much too quickly. Sam Bayard told me that the magic words were the fiddler saying, "Now let's see about those old tunes you wanted," or something to that effect. At that point the fiddler would dust off his instrument, rosin his bow, and begin playing. That was the objective of my visit in the first place.

As a fiddler played his tunes I took notes. I noted the tune's title, the key in which he played it, and anything else fiddlers had to say about particular tunes. As standard questions I would ask: who were his favorite fiddlers; where did he learn specific tunes; did he like to play square dances; did he travel to bluegrass and/or fiddlers' conventions; did he like to swap tunes; did he use the radio, television, or records to learn tunes; what were some other titles for the tunes he played; and were there many local or regional tune titles.

I sought fiddlers from any source available to me. I received referrals from the fiddlers themselves, tips from friends, parents, and people I randomly questioned around the towns. It was easy to introduce myself to a fiddler and his family because I was a musician interested in learning old-fashioned fiddle tunes. When I was referred by other players, I always crossed my fingers because I never knew how well they got along with each other. Nevertheless, this technique proved so effective that I found only two players in the Buffalo Valley by myself: Joe Bell and Ralph Sauers, whose son, John, worked with my father.

Matthew and I recorded the fiddlers of the Buffalo Valley in order to learn as many tunes as possible. We learned that a clear recording of a fiddler's tunes was essential, especially when we encountered the ordeal of making transcriptions. The better the recording the better chance Matthew had of making a good transcription. With some players like David Bell and Marvin Kratzer even the clearest recording could not eliminate the challenge of transcribing their music from tape to paper.

The trick to making a good recording is the placement of the players around the microphone(s). In a fiddler's living room if everyone crowds around the microphone, the result will be simply a recording of oldtime or bluegrass music. While this is fun, it was not exactly what we were after. There is too much music to deal with, and it is practically impossible to sort out the notes of a fiddle tune when it is obscured by so much accompaniment. Here are some guidelines which may prove helpful:

1. The microphone must be as close to the fiddler as possible with the record levels monitored. This results in a clear recording and consequently a clear reproduction of his tunes.

2. Two people should go on a recording interview so that one can conduct the interview while the other monitors the recording levels.

3. Keep the backtime musicians facing the fiddler, but place the microphone(s) squarely in front of the fiddler. The tape recorder will record the backtime playing but not at the expense of the fiddler's tune. A distance of four to five feet between the fiddler and the backtime musicians should suffice.

4. Use the best tape recorder available. If a two-track recorder is used, use one track for the fiddler and one for the backtime.

5. Make a duplicate for the fiddler and his family, and make sure he knows where the original is going.

6. Announce the tune and the key if possible.

Backtime is a term which refers to musical accompaniment and is commonplace among fiddle players. With its chordal "fill" and rhythmic consistency, the guitar serves as the very best backtime instrument. I like to accompany fiddlers with my banjo too, especially in the frailing* or clawhammer style. Regardless of the backtime instrument used, I believe that a fiddler, especially a square dance fiddler, needs to lead the music. While he enjoys the sound of his own instrument solo, he appreciates the strength of accompanying instruments such as the guitar, banjo, or bass.

Backtime serves another purpose. When playing at home, fiddlers occasionally play irregularly. They frequently add measures, fancy endings, and tempo changes at the expense of the rhythmic integrity and regularity of the fiddle tune. Accompaniment tends to regularize playing. It helps eliminate extra measures, tempo changes, and other irregularities while discouraging a fiddler from excessive experimentation in technique. It also assists him in finding the notes on his instrument—a fiddle has no frets to guide the player to the correct notes.

Backtime has a drawback. Pitch becomes standardized rather than being fluid. Intonational variation, common in both instrumental and sung Anglo-American folk music, seems to be lost or permanently amended by the standardized frets of the guitar and even the banjo. This tends to force a fiddler to standardize his own tones. Consequently, many of the fiddle's "neutral tones" are lost. Regardless of the ill-effects of backtime on the tonal integrity of fiddle tunes, being able to accompany a fiddler can make a collecting session more enjoyable and musically more rewarding.

Rapport begins with the establishment of a relationship based on a mutual interest like music. Developing such rapport was a major undertaking, and it served as a yardstick by which I measured the success we achieved with each fiddler we met. The fiddlers were our teachers, and we listened to them intently. In time, Matthew and I became familiar faces to the fiddlers and their families. Often

*See the Glossary for the definition of this term and other musical terms.

interviews and recording sessions became family parties where everyone participated to one degree or another.

When a fiddler we hoped to interview could not afford the time we wished to spend with him, often due to family commitments, we turned to another fiddler. I disliked returning home from a trip with nothing to show for my efforts, so when someone was not home or was unavailable I would drop in for a short visit with someone else. After all, these fiddlers quickly became friends. Laura Bell said once, "Oh, Bob, I knew you were coming today; I just knew." It is heartwarming to be so welcome even when you just drop in.

The collection which Matthew and I pieced together is still growing. From its beginning on September 15, 1973, when I met Joe Bell in Penns Creek and made tape number 1, the collection has expanded to over forty-four cassettes and reels of fiddlers mostly from the Buffalo Valley. The materials of our collection are in the Pattee Library of The Pennsylvania State University. Copies of the field tapes are also in the Archive of Folksong, Library of Congress, Music Division, Washington, D.C.

I would like to take this opportunity to direct the reader's attention to MacEdward Leach's and Henry Glassie's *A Field Guide for Collectors of Oral Traditions and Folk Cultural Material in Pennsylvania* (Harrisburg: Pennsylvania Historical and Museum Commission, 1973) and Kenneth Goldstein's *A Guide for Field Workers in Folklore* (Hatboro, Pa.: Folklore Associates, 1964). Both these books shed light on the collecting problem and help answer the many questions one might have about how to go about identifying and collecting folk materials.

I hope you enjoy this book. From beginning to end it has been a great challenge to those of us directly involved. From the field trips where we met fiddlers and their families to listening sessions with Professor Bayard, to fiddlers' competitions each summer, the vast storehouse of folk music around us has become an integral part of our lives. As the fiddlers of the Buffalo Valley shared their music with us, so we are pleased to share it again with you.

1

Fiddling: An Overview

Fiddling is one of the oldest and most common folk music forms in the United States, the British Isles, and Europe. Through hundreds of years of almost uninterrupted popularity, styles, repertoires, and even the instrument itself have changed. Folk instruments of the fiddle or violin type existed in many early cultures. Since the sixteenth century the fiddle as we now know it has been both a folk and fine art instrument. Its folk application, or fiddling, is our major concern. In Chapter 3 we will look closely at some of the attitudinal, stylistic, and technical differences between fiddling and violin playing.

American fiddling was imported in great part from Ireland, Scotland, and England. The dance-related styles and tunes of fiddlers, so much a part of folk culture, were carried by emigrants to their new American homeland. As they settled throughout this huge country, their folk culture gradually developed regional variants. These regional variations in fiddling style occur extensively throughout the United States, especially along the Appalachian range. Here the mountains mark the line along which settlement first extended and act as barriers to communication and travel. The resulting isolation has led to the development and maintenance of regional stylistic phenomena. From maritime Canada and New England through New York, Pennsylvania, West Virginia, Virginia, Kentucky, Tennessee, and the Carolinas to Georgia, styles and repertoires gradually change. Of course, differences are most apparent between the geographical extremes.

In New England, the survival of the Irish origins is seen most clearly. Most tunes are comprised of single notes; only occasionally are double stops and drones introduced. The bowing renders these notes clear and well defined. Jigs, hornpipes, and clogs have remained popular along with reels. As one moves south, fiddling sounds heavier, or more rugged. Emphasis is on droning and double stopping. Bowing is patterned and very rhythmic. With regard to repertoire, the jigs, hornpipes, and clogs common in New England give way almost entirely to square dance-style reels.

Moving from one region toward another, gradual changes in style and repertoire are noticeable. In Virginia, tunes and styles are similar to those in neighboring areas, while in New York, practices are like those of New England fiddlers. Within a particular state, subregional styles may have developed. Fiddling in southwestern Pennsylvania, hardly distinguishable from fiddling in northern West Virginia, clearly differs from the playing in the southeastern part of Pennsylvania. In the central part of the state, a combination of stylistic elements from areas to the north and to the south has yielded an identifiable hybrid. The Buffalo Valley, in central Pennsylvania, harbors an interesting subregional style. Bowing among the oldtime players there is rhythmic, patterned, and repetitious, and one frequently hears drones and double stops. Jigs and reels, along with schottisches, polkas, and waltzes, are all still played, though the popularity of the German dance pieces has begun to diminish. In Chapter 5 we will meet one of the Buffalo Valley's oldtime players, examining his style, techniques, and tunes, and we will try to make some generalizations about square dance players and their art.

The tunes played in a given area are to a certain extent an expression of regionalism. Each area has a core repertoire common to most of the players. This is not to suggest that tunes found in one area will not be played in another, only that the repertoires of fiddlers within a region will overlap more than will the repertoires of players from different regions. Even within an area, however, each fiddler will play certain pieces that only he knows while other of his tunes will be familiar to practically all players.

Tune names also seem to be fairly consistent within, yet variable between, geographic regions. In the Buffalo Valley, "Soldier's Joy" is the name of a tune which in other parts of the country occasionally carries the title "King's Head" or "French Four." "Flop-Eared Mule" is known in other areas as "Nigger in the

Woodpile" or "Monkey in the Barber Shop." Even though titles do vary, one can notice consistency of repertoire within a particular region because of the regularity regarding tune names within that area.

Regionalism is gradually becoming less apparent as mass media more and more homogenize traditional music. Both styles and repertoires fall prey to a standardizing influence. Fiddlers adjust their playing to match tune versions heard on television, radio, and records. In this way the media shape playing styles and at the same time expose musicians to a greater variety of styles and tunes.

The strongest challenge to the regional integrity of fiddling is bluegrass music. Cutting across geographic boundaries, bluegrass has had a significant impact on the tunes and techniques of traditional players. Born in Kentucky in the 1930s through the almost single-handed efforts of Bill Monroe, bluegrass has developed its own styles and repertoires. In its early years, bluegrass quickly received commercial attention from the radio and recording industries. When traditional players heard it on the radio, they were fascinated. In the Buffalo Valley it has altered traditional styles and repertoires more than any other recent musical phenomenon. How bluegrass differs from oldtime fiddling and the new techniques it has introduced are the subject of Chapter 6. We will look at the playing of one bluegrass fiddler and try to define what bluegrass is.

Bluegrass has contributed in many ways to the deterioration of regionalism. Each year hundreds of bluegrass festivals are held throughout the country. Drawing together players from different areas, festivals expose folk musicians to a variety of tunes and techniques they might never have heard otherwise. After learning from other players who attend, fiddlers carry their discoveries home where they in turn pass them on.

This is the mode of transmission in any folk art. Folk music is maintained and passed on solely by its practitioners. No written collections of tunes or "how to" books assure the art's survival; that is in the hands of the fiddlers. Though printed collections of tunes are not uncommon, and often players who read music will learn pieces from them, the survival of folk art depends on aural maintenance and transmission.

When passed from one player to the next, fiddling invariably picks up individual peculiarities. As these differences and innovations are passed on, tunes and styles gradually and constantly evolve. By transmission over a period of several generations, tunes and techniques can change dramatically. Each generation impresses its stamp, a work of its era, on tradition. In Chapter 4 we look at two fiddlers who have grown too old to play much anymore. During their active playing years, these fiddlers were exposed to some unique influences. These influences passed, and the traditional tunes and techniques survived more or less intact, attesting to the durability of folk fiddling traditions.

Despite this constant evolution, folk music retains an amazing consistency. For folk music to survive and be taught to succeeding generations, it must contain certain static elements which can be learned. As a result, those elements that are fundamental to the art change very slowly. Peripheral qualities which result from individual innovations are not fundamental to the art and thus may fade or change more quickly. In Chapter 3 we are concerned with the basic elements of fiddling and how they are learned. Though this learning process is difficult to examine, we may find something in it which helps keep fiddling so consistent through the years.

Transmission from generation to generation is carried on, to a great extent, within musical or tradition-bearing families. Parents who play music teach their children to play. We found that most of our fiddlers came from families whose members played some kind of instrument. Learning to appreciate music at home, they had early guidance and instruction. Later their own children in turn took up the family's music. In Chapter 7 the Bell family offers a good example of the "musical family." All the children are interested in their father's playing and are learning instruments that allow the family to play together in a complementary fashion.

Collecting fiddle tunes helps preserve a fragment of a continuing tradition. Many have noted that folk art is declining in the wake of influences from mass media and urban civilization. The rural bastions of traditions are falling. Preoccupied with what they see and hear on television and radio, people are allowing their folk traditions to slip away. Periodic revivals, such as the recent resurgence of folk music in the late fifties and early sixties, occasionally direct attention to folk art forms, but nonetheless, fewer fiddlers come forward each year to carry on the tradition.

In our collecting project, Bob Doyle and I felt it was important to preserve more than just a tiny portion of the fiddler's repertoire. We wanted to preserve a picture of each player's personality and environment as well—a record of the intimate bond between a player's personality, home, and music. I hope the rapport we developed with these fiddlers will be evident in the interviews and discussions. All participated in an experience that was mutually enjoyed by the players, their families, and us.

2

The Buffalo Valley and Its Fiddlers

The Buffalo Valley runs east–west in Central Pennsylvania for about fifty miles. Mountains surround the valley on the north, south, and west. The Susquehanna and Jacks mountains to the south; and Bald Eagle to the west. The Susquehanna River closes the valley at the east, taking the flow of the valley's two major streams, Penns and Buffalo creeks. Three major highways serve the valley. Routes 45 and 192 run east–west while routes 11 and 15 travel north–south hugging the Susquehanna River. Though most are now paved, many smaller roads and lanes are still dirt or gravel.

Farms, woodlands, and small towns make up the Buffalo Valley. Neither Lewisburg, the Union County seat, nor nearby Middleburg, in Snyder County, is very large, and on the whole, the valley's rural character remains undisturbed. In summer the valley is carpeted with a deep green. Before the hay is cut, baled, and stored, some farmers take advantage of their empty barns to hold square dances. Not long ago square dancing seemed to be dying out, but recently it has enjoyed a new popularity. With this renewed interest, fiddlers now have opportunities to display their talents and perhaps make a little money.

New Berlin, the home of one of our fiddlers, is a typical Buffalo Valley town. It can be identified from a distance by the spire of the church at the town's center.

Photo courtesy of *Union County Journal*

Old, white houses are set back from the wide main street. Looking closely, one may find a weed-covered hitching post, a relic of an era bygone in years but not in spirit.

Change comes slowly in the Buffalo Valley. Urban morality finds resistance. Penetrating the isolation, the mass media have yet to rifle the valley's conservatism. Aware of current trends, the valley's people do inch toward modernity, but with little enthusiasm. While ultimately it did not turn out to be a hindrance for our fiddlers, my long hair drew more than one suspicious glance.

Pennsylvania was settled valley by valley. Two nationalities dominated the Buffalo Valley's settlement and hence ethnic composition. Immigrants from the British Isles were first to arrive almost two centuries ago. The Germans were not far behind. German is still a second language to many. German word order, phrasing,

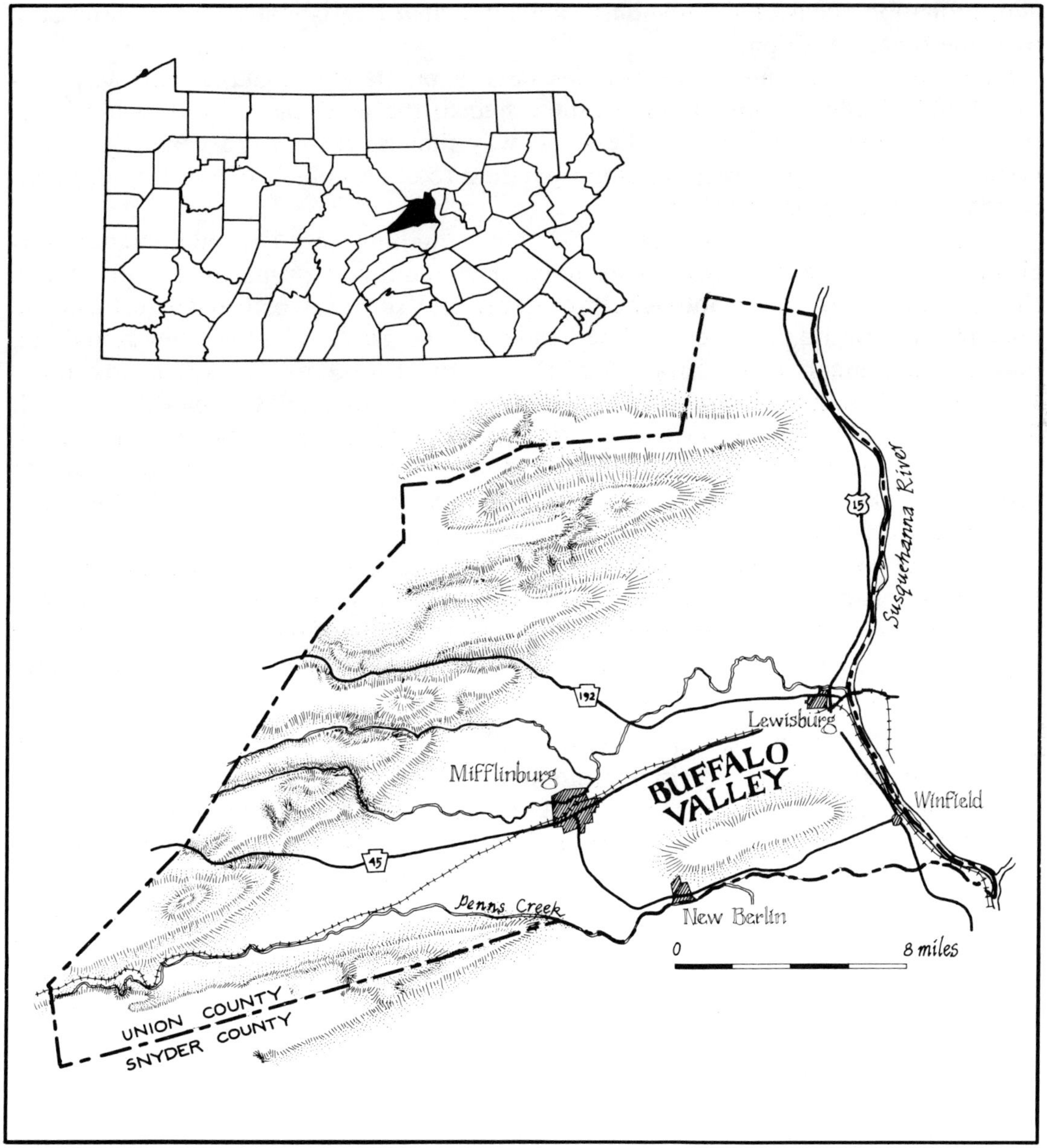

BUFFALO VALLEY
Lewisburg
Mifflinburg
Winfield
New Berlin
Penns Creek
Susquehanna River
15
192
45
0
8 miles
UNION COUNTY
SNYDER COUNTY

and intonation occasionally invade English in a characteristically "jumped the cow over the fence" fashion.

Since the 1950s, Amish communities have been steadily making their way into the Buffalo Valley adding another ethnic hue to the landscape. Clothed in black, the Amish plow their fields in the same way their ancestors did years ago, their horse-drawn carriages creeping along winding roads mindless of the traffic which builds impatiently behind them.

Despite the German character of the valley, fiddling here is predominantly Anglo-Scots-Irish. German influences have been confined primarily to repertoire, though now, even the schottisches, waltzes, and polkas which used to form the bulk of the round dances seem to be headed to the grave with their few remaining players and dancers (see Chapter 5). Other types of folklore—tales, legends, pow-wowing, and faith healing—are still preserved in both their German and British forms. Especially among those of German extraction, spells and bewitching arouse fears and expectations. Astronomical and weather signs are often consulted to predict the likelihood of success or failure in a variety of endeavors like building, planting, and fishing.

Historical legends flourish. Stories of battles between the early settlers and the Indians are handed from generation to generation. Throughout our interviews, Ralph Sauers, one of our inactive fiddlers, told us many of the valley's legends and tales (see Chapter 4). From his enthusiasm one might easily believe he was there when what he described happened.

Ralph: And the buffalo path that you was talkin' about, mebbe you heard about the buffalo path back there in the mountain? Well, back at Sand Bridge, in the 14-mile-an-hour road, is a path that comes on the north side of the mountain, comes up over, jumps a swamp, and comes down by the side. Now they said that that path was worn in by the buffaloes crossin' the mountains over in Buffalo Valley, where they grazed over there and fed. And back there in Forest Hill during Indian days was a mill. And the Indians attacked that mill one day. There was two men in the mill. They run from the mill. One stumbled and fell, and the Indians shot him, they did. But that guy who didn't fall, the bullets went over top of him and he made it. Now, if you get back to our early settlers and stuff, I think just around here, the most interesting would be at this spot, would be the Leroy Massacre back here.

Bob: Were there any survivors?

Ralph: Yeah, from what I heard, they carried a girl off, clear out to Ohio she was took. It was a big Indian village out there. But they fetched her back one way or another, and got her back again. She walked there, too. That's the only way they traveled in them days.

Did ya ever hear about bewitching?

Bob: Yes, a little bit. I don't understand it. Explain it.

Ralph: Well, they claim that back in the old days, everybody believed in witches and hexes. They claimed that they had super powers. They could do this and that. My grandfather believed in that stuff. But what happened, he went wherever he was workin', it was the fall of the year. And he told the neighbors what he had seen. And one of them said, "We'll put a stop to that all right." He said they had to butcher a bull that had horns. And one fella went and worked this bull hide over him and around him in some way or another so he represented the devil. And every night they went in there and told that woman and girl if they wouldn't quit that stuff, they'd take care of them. That was the last of that stuff. Now, that's about your hex'n' and hexes that the old people believed. They had all kinds of beliefs . . . well, some of the beliefs was, if you'd go out and put an X over your barn door, the hexes (witches) couldn't get in. They claimed that if your cow was behexed—if a cow gave bloody milk—they said that the cow was behexed. And some of them would go out and paint big X's on their barns and stuff.

Bob: Where did the hexes live?

Ralph: Well, they could live anyplace. They could be your next-door-neighbor.

Bob: How did the people tell the weather around here? Are there any signs for the weather?

Ralph: Oh, yes, them old fellas—now my granddaddy was a carpenter. In the moon, if you look into a good almanac, the old *Lancaster* was your best one and I don't know if they're printin' that now or not. Yeh, they went by the moon for a lot of stuff. Now, as I said, my granddaddy was a carpenter, and they wouldn't nail a shingle roof on if it was the dark side of the moon.*

Bob: Why? What did they say?

Ralph: The shingles would turn up.

*Ralph seems to have it backwards on this point. As I understand it, the dark of the moon or, more exactly, the waning moon was the time to nail shingles.

The Buffalo Valley is rich in many kinds of folklore but Bob and I confined our collecting to fiddle music. Both old time and bluegrass fiddling are fairly common. Square dancing is still popular and gives dance fiddlers a chance to perform. In addition, several bluegrass ensembles play throughout the valley, exposing traditional fiddlers to bluegrass's stylistic peculiarities. Let us turn to some general characteristics of fiddling.

3

Fiddling Style: Rhythmic Bowing and Melodic Ornamentation

As a fiddler I have often been asked what the difference is between a violin and a fiddle. Many people do not realize they are the same instrument. Some fiddlers may slightly alter the shape of the bridge—flattening it helps in the execution of drones and double stops—but what really differentiates the two is the way they are played. The whiney rhythmic sounds of the fiddle are quite different from the violin's sweet tones. As a folk art, fiddling differs on many counts from violin playing, a fine art. The attitude of the musician toward his art, the attitude of the audience toward both the musician and his art, and the learning process for each are three major points which distinguish violin playing from fiddling.

Fiddlers and violinists usually play in different settings. At home on a back porch, informal concert, or square dance, the fiddler performs in a more relaxed atmosphere than the concert violinist. Violin performances are usually more formal than fiddle performances where a certain casual air has conjured for many people a "knee-slapping" image of fiddlers and fiddling.

A good violinist is far more particular about his sound than is a square dance fiddler. Exactness in noting, richness in tone, and smoothness of delivery are essential to the trained violinist. The violinist is also more likely to demand that a high standard be maintained by his fellow artists.

Orchestral playing requires uniformity. To assure homogeneity, each violinist in a section must play his part exactly as it is written. The notes and parts are not approximate but precise. All players must conform. They are not at liberty to abridge passages or flat occasional tones as is the folk fiddler.

Fiddlers seldom play in large groups with other fiddlers but when they do, it has been my experience that most play without particular regard for uniformity. Each offers his own rendition of the tune, disregarding inconsistencies and irregularities. The result is not as cacophonous as one might expect. Fiddle tunes are usually simple harmonically and most players' renditions have the same basic melody at heart. Additionally, many of the ornaments each employs are similar to or the same as other players' ornaments. The result is a more or less coherent tune peppered with harmonies and dissonances. Intonational inconsistencies among a group of fiddlers, as in an orchestra, are swallowed by an averaging effect.

The fiddler seems to perceive his art differently from the violinist. He is generally less critical. His intonation is often approximate and his tone can be very inconsistent. "Scratchiness," or even "screeching" is not nearly as offensive to the fiddler as it is to the violinist.

Fiddlers usually play solo or with the accompaniment of guitars, banjos, mandolins, and basses. The fiddler in such an ensemble must maintain a cadence and approximate a tune melody. Beyond that, he may ornament freely. If he should make a mistake or drop or add a beat, the accompanying musicians adapt to the irregularity without challenging the fiddler's lead.

The relationship between the artist and the audience also differentiates the folk performer from the fine art performer. Folk performances are usually more casual and relaxed than are fine art performances. This casualness is apparent in both the player's attitude and the attitude of the audience.

Though many solo violinists may directly address the audience, there is a formality to the interaction which can hardly go unnoticed. The audience, in general, has the expectation of entering into a cultural experience. Their chief, if not only, form of communication with the performer is applause. For instance, one would never find the audience clapping along with a sonata. The artist often adds to the air of formality by dressing in tails or at least a tuxedo. Though this picture is stereotypical and simplistic, I think it makes the important point that fine art performances are less casual than folk art performances.

The typical performing situation for the folk fiddler is the square dance. The fiddler's musical accomplishment is far outweighed by the overall danceability of the fiddler's ensemble and the caller's creativity and articulation. How well the fiddler plays is a function of how appropriate his playing is for dancing. The technical demands being therefore less than those required of the violinist, the fiddler's art requires less concentration. Some of the more specific requirements of dance fiddling will be the focus of Chapter 5.

The violinist seems more to be playing for an audience, whereas the fiddler seems to play with the audience. The fiddler is one of the people he is playing for. He is often a member of the local community. He may know many of the members of the audience personally. At intermission he mingles freely with the dancers. The

violinist, on the other hand, is not as likely to be a member of the community he is playing for. His acquaintances in the audience are bound to be fewer and his personal interaction is likely to be more restricted. The whole point is, of course, that folk art and fine art differ with respect to performing situations, and that the attitudes of the performers and audiences toward the art itself are different as well.

The Learning Process

The violin is certainly one of the most difficult instruments to master. The student of classical violin faces a highly regimented program of instruction under the tutorial guidance of an accomplished artist. The techniques of classical playing are carefully defined, assuring uniformity in the art. Fiddlers, on the other hand, subscribe to no such rote. Since the way one learns to fiddle is not meticulously spelled out, the beginner himself must isolate those qualities which are characteristic of fiddling and seek to reproduce them in his own playing.

Few people have trouble differentiating fiddling from violin playing; consequently, someone wishing to learn how to fiddle should be able to easily identify practitioners of the art form he wishes to master. After finding several examples on which to base his playing, the novice must embark upon some sort of learning procedure. Since instruction is bound to be informal and intermittent at best, the way one acquires the skill is much harder to study. As a fiddler myself, I understand intuitively what skills must be mastered in order to fiddle. During our study I wondered whether other fiddlers developed these skills in the same way I had. As the rapport with our fiddlers improved, I began to ask how they had learned to play.

Examining the experiences of our fiddlers, together with my own, I isolated three distinct steps in the learning process:

1. Initial introduction to and acquaintance with the instrument.
2. The development of specific bowing techniques and patterns to effect rhythmic punctuation.
3. The incorporation of ornamentation into simple tune lines to vary and enliven basic melodies.

After one successfully incorporates step 2 into his playing, he can claim to be a fiddler. Step 3 is a somewhat advanced technique which allows for continued growth.

Introduction to the Instrument

The violin has no frets. Sound is produced by drawing the tightened hair of a bow across strings which are supported by a wooden bridge standing between the F holes. The first problem confronting the beginner is that of producing a specific, clear tone. I remember my own hair-tearing efforts at trying to play even the

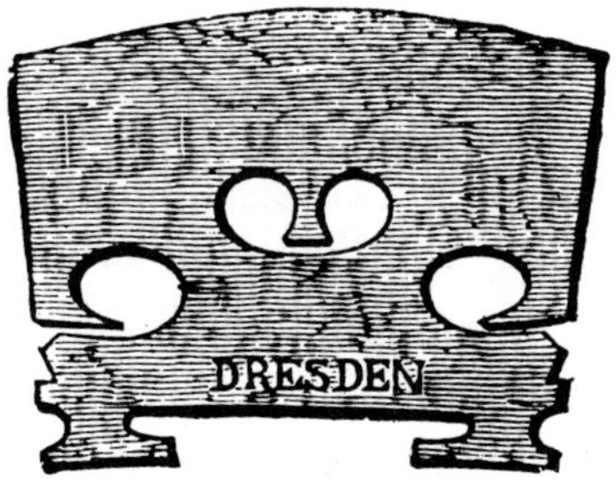

simplest melodies. My first attempts centered around melodies like "Mary Had a Little Lamb" and "Twinkle Twinkle Little Star." Nonplayers have no idea how hard it is to first find the notes of a melody, and then play them with even minimal clarity. To progress, however, a fiddler must overcome this initial challenge.

Bob asked Marvin Kratzer, one of our bluegrass fiddlers and the subject of Chapter 6, about his first encounter with the fiddle. Explaining that he had so much trouble with bowing, Marvin picked out tunes on a mandolin because it has the same relative fingering as the fiddle. Here are excerpts from that interview:

Marvin: So I started playing it on the mandolin. I played the mandolin before and got all the finger work out on it—played the notes out on the neck.

Bob: Did anyone show you how to play the mandolin?

Marvin: No, I played by ear. I kept at it till I got the sound I wanted to play. I couldn't get the bow when I started, so I picked it [the fiddle] like a mandolin. [Picking, Marvin then played "Old Grey Mare."]

The Old Gray Mare—version one

Bob: Then what?

Marvin: That's the way I played it so I got on to the bow and got there.* [Bowing, Marvin played the version over again.] I played like that for a month or so and started getting a little better and got into double stopping. So I kept at it and kept at it a while and started playing a little faster, and it sounded like this [version 2].

*Marvin usually bows each note as he did in this rendition.

The Old Gray Mare—version two

Anyone hearing Marvin Kratzer describe his progress might think it took him only about three weeks of intensive practice, but, be assured, it was a long, tedious process. When I first met Marvin he told me that he had been playing since he was eighteen years old. At the time of this interview he was thirty-nine. It did not require a month or so as Marvin stated. Instead he actually spent the first few years coping with what is essentially step 1. It took quite a while until Marvin discovered how to get the "sound" he wanted.

The Need for Rhythmic Bowing

No matter how well they can execute the fingering, most fiddlers are not happy being able to play only simple tunes like "Old Grey Mare." There is a "sound" which lures these musicians, a sound which they must develop. The fiddling "sound" I refer to is a result of many musical qualities. Rhythmic bowing plays an important role; so does droning of open strings, occasional double stops, use of slightly sharped or flatted tones, and frequent glissando starting either a half or a quarter step above or below the note desired and sliding into it. Frequently, achieving this goal requires assistance. Marvin recruited help from several fiddlers. By observing them and listening intently to the type of playing he wished to learn, he soon noticed the importance of rhythmic bowing.

Offering an experience of my own, I recall sitting in my apartment one afternoon playing "Oh Suzanna" when a fellow (Peter Schwimmer) visiting friends next door stopped to see who was "screeching" away on the fiddle. He turned out to be a bluegrass banjo picker and fiddler. I asked him to play a tune, so he picked up my

scroll
peg
nut
fingerboard
bridge
'f' hole
tailpiece
chinrest
endpin

fiddle and sawed out "Turkey in the Straw." Clearly above my ability at the time, he offered a lesson which I hastily accepted.

The very first thing I noticed about Pete's playing was that it was extremely rhythmic. The bow moved furiously over the strings producing that familiar drive so characteristic of fiddling. Close scrutiny revealed that his "Turkey in the Straw" was built around the rhythmic sequence  . Each note of this sequence he bowed individually, creating a bowing pattern which consisted of one long stroke and two short strokes. Between sequences, the long stroke alternated from an up stroke to a down stroke. After studying Pete's playing, I attempted to learn this bowing pattern. To firmly ingrain this rhythmic pattern, I repeatedly bowed the sequence until it became smooth and relaxed. That the long stroke alternated from up to down seemed to be the biggest obstacle to fluidity.

I discovered that many tunes can be bowed almost entirely without deviating from this pattern, or at least they can be squeezed into conforming to it. A problem does arise, however, when  is abbreviated to  or expanded to  in order to render a melodic passage more effectively. In the first case, the pattern is broken by two long strokes which have to be bowed successively  . The other variation requires that the second sixteenth note be either slurred in the same stroke with the first or bowed separately ( or ). Since four sixteenth notes can be slurred together in one stroke, bowed individually, or divided into groups of two, it is only essential that the lilt established by the initial sequence be maintained. My one-lesson teacher preferred to slur the second of the four sixteenth notes with the first, and bow the other two. This retains the alternation of the long stroke from up to down and continues a bowing pattern. Most of our players usually bow each of the notes in such a sequence managing easily to preserve the cadence and rhythmic punctuation.

After he understands basic rhythmic requirements and realizes how to achieve them, a fiddler must develop fluid bowing. To bow smoothly demands very particular arm and wrist movements. Most of the to and fro motion is accomplished with the shoulder and elbow in a sawing motion. Since such arm movement alone will result in an ever-changing bow direction as the elbow and shoulder move in an arc, the wrist and fingers must help compensate to keep the bow traveling perpendicular to the strings. They can also help smooth changes in bow direction. At the

end of each stroke the fingers and wrist should be moved so that they lead and guide the bow. In this way, the bow is pulled, in a certain sense, even during an up bow. Such a developed use of the fingers and wrist is not especially common among the "average" square dance player but is rather an accomplishment of more advanced fiddlers. The fingers and wrist can also provide definition and lilt to the notes by applying subtle pressures to the bow. Rhythm is predominantly physical in nature and in fiddling is expressed through the bow. The fiddler must establish a tempo that takes over his entire body. In other words, he must immerse himself in the rhythm.

A few years ago I had the good fortune of meeting Bob Cheeseman, a fiddler from whom I learned several tunes. Since Bob had started out as a violinist, he already had a basic knowledge of fingering and bowing when he decided to learn to fiddle. He quickly found that playing the violin was quite different from fiddling. To fiddle, one has to learn the necessary bowing techniques. Familiar with the melodies of elementary fiddle tunes, Bob eventually stumbled across the same bowing techniques and rhythmic patterns that I had. I asked Bob Cheeseman how he learned to fiddle. Here are portions of that conversation:

Bob Cheeseman: For me that was really something. For me to take it straight, and then get the fiddle bow into it.

Matthew: What was your progress? What did you start doing first?

Bob Cheeseman [First played and then continued talking]: Now that was old "One Little, Two Little, Three Little Indians," which is where you really first get that action of the bow and try to get the wrist into it. That's a hard thing to come by when you're not used to it!

One Little, Two Little, Three Little Indians

Bob's rendition of this simple melody is totally dominated by the rhythmic sequence  . This is the same rhythmic pattern which I had noticed dominated Pete's playing and which I had tried to learn myself. Bob isolated, in its simplest form, that quality which to him most distinguished fiddling from violin playing, the "fiddle bow," as he called it. He then went on to develop his playing further.

Ornamentation

Fiddlers often ornament the melody or rhythm of a tune. It is not unusual for a fiddler to render a tune slightly differently each time he plays it. Though a tune may be dominated by a rhythmic sequence like  , other rhythms, and therefore other bowings, may be incorporated into a tune version. As was noted in the previous section,  may be abbreviated to  or expanded to  and then bowed in a number of ways. Each way a sequence is bowed will yield a slightly different rhythm. Likewise, a fiddler may melodically embellish a simple passage in order to enliven and individualize his version. Fiddle tunes usually have fairly simple tune lines. As long as the basic shape of a melody is maintained, certain note sequences can be substituted for others without jeopardizing the coherence of the tune.

The art of substituting one group of notes for another is a technique which one can learn. This ability not only demonstrates a command over and comprehension of the melody, it also forces the fiddler to learn new techniques in order to play the alterations he desires. Most fiddlers become aware of ornamentation at the same time they begin to learn fundamental bowing patterns and techniques. A fiddler might replace a note sequence with one that allows for the continuance of a specific bowing pattern. When a fiddler has reached the point where he can vary his bowing somewhat, his potential for melodic variation increases.

How and when a fiddler learns to ornament is not easy to determine. Such skills are acquired partly through exposure to tunes that are mere assemblages of ornamentation. Hearing tune versions which have been elaborately embellished by other fiddlers is another source of reference and inspiration. Exactly how and why a particular tune is ornamented is frequently not understood by the fiddler himself. While consciously attempted, ornamentation is not based on a developed understanding of theory; it grows out of a desire to enhance a particular tune and an ability to summon forth ornamental formulas which can be appropriately employed in a variety of melodic or rhythmic situations. Interviewing David Bell, the subject of Chapter 7, I asked him about several of his tune versions and how he developed them.

Matthew: Would you play "The Girl I Left behind Me" as simply as you can?
David: [Plays version one.]

The Girl I Left behind Me—version one

Matthew: Now play a real fancy version.
David: [Plays an ornate version; version two is only the first half of the tune.]

The Girl I Left behind Me—version two

Matthew: You are the only person I've ever heard who plays it that well. Do you know any other tunes that you "soup-up" like that? How about "Buffalo Gals," real simple?

David: [Plays two versions.]

Matthew: Would you do something like that for "Marching Through Georgia"? Or do you play that straight?

David: That would be straight.

Matthew: What about "Redwing"?

David: That'd be the same.

Matthew: Can you think of any other tunes that are like that?

David: Some of them's one way, and some you can jazz up.

Matthew: "Maple Sugar" you can jazz up kind of.

David: No, that's about the same all the way through.

Bob: How do you figure out how you jazz them up?

Matthew: Well, how did you play "The Girl I Left behind Me" the first time you played it?

David: Oh, I don't remember the way I used to play it any more. [David plays the simple version he first played, then the second one again.]

Matthew: How did you figure out how to do that?

David: I just run onto it, that's all.

Matthew: Did you try to do it?

David: Yeah, I was pissing with the fiddle one day, just monkeying around and come onto it. [David played the elaborate version again.]

Matthew: That's pretty much your own version then, isn't it?

Buffalo Gals—version one

Buffalo Gals—version two

David: Yeah.

Matthew: You have a pretty fancy version of "The Eighth of January" too; did you learn that pretty simple at first?

David: Well, I learned it off Elmer Shaffer.

David: [Plays the first half of "The Eighth of January."]

The Eighth of January—version one

The Eighth of January—version two

Matthew: Now give us an example of your licks.

David: [Plays version two.] Elmer usually plays it more straight.

Matthew: How about the "Arkansas Traveller"? That's one too that you can jazz up or play straight.

David: No, that's about the same all the way through.

One can see that tunes are often shaped by the fiddler. He may take a tune that has a plain melody and ornament it into a complex, individualized version. "The Girl I Left Behind," "Buffalo Gals," and "The Eighth of January" were all learned by David in a simple form and later embellished. Other tunes do not inspire ornamentation and remain basically unchanged in a fiddler's repertoire. "Maple Sugar," "Redwing," and "Arkansas Traveller" never went through David's individualizing process. This is not to suggest, as David seemed to, that they resist being ornamented; rather, each fiddler tries to embellish either pieces that particularly appeal to him or tunes that contain melodic strains especially vulnerable to the ornamental formulas at his command. To demonstrate that a tune like "Arkansas Traveller" can in fact be easily ornamented, I offer transcriptions of two versions. Because the point can be adequately made with only the first half of the tune, I did not include a complete transcription.

We have yet to examine how a fiddler learns to ornament a tune. David says that he just "ran onto it." Although he consciously attempted to alter tunes from the way he first learned them, he could not articulate precisely why or how he had done so. Going back to Bob Cheeseman, I asked why and how he ornamented certain tunes.

Matthew: But when you put the runs into it, into the basic melody for "Buffalo Gals," when you really get going, that's what I'm curious about, how you figured out what to play.

Bob Cheeseman: I just felt my way into it. See, this is where you have the advantage because you've been playing by ear where I've been going by the written score, and it just had to come out, and it had to come out right. I don't know, there probably are other ways you can finger it, but that's the way I came up with it. I started out with just that. [Bob played the bare melody.] Which is the way it was really written, and then I started this with the fiddle bow, then I started to get these groups of four into it. I just had to work it out where it sounded right. [Plays the ornamented version.]

Arkansas Traveler—simple

Arkansas Traveler—ornamented

Matthew: You should play bluegrass.

Bob Cheeseman: But the thing is it doesn't come that easy for me. Another old-timer, well I'll play it up where I started to, that was "Golden Slippers."

Matthew: Did you work up a version for that?

Bob Cheeseman: Yeah, I've known that tune for years and believe I've seen it written, but I don't remember, but I started playing it, I mean really picking it up, by ear.

Matthew: Go through the same way with "Golden Slippers."

Bob Cheeseman: Well, all right. If I can get the basic tune of it now. [Plays the tune.] Of course that's simple fingering. All I did was take the straight tune and fiddle bow it without trying to put any fingering in it.

Matthew: Did you ever try to put any fingering in it?

Bob Cheeseman: No, I never have on that one because it's . . . I would rather go

Buffalo Gals—version one

the double stop on it without trying to put in any fingering. [Bob did not double stop or drone in this version.]

Matthew: I tried putting fingering in it.

Bob Cheeseman: I don't think it lends itself to it because you've got an odd rhythm there. It's not really the same. If you look at the score of that sometime, your eighth notes are in there, and it doesn't quite lend itself, but it's easy to double stop.*

Unusual as it may seem, Bob Cheeseman, like David Bell, was not quite sure how he developed his particular versions. The "groups of four" sixteenth notes which replaced eighth-note passages fit into the basic melodic structure very easily, yet why he chose some ornaments over others escaped him.

Bob Cheeseman suggested that ornamentation is a skill which, in part, depends on learning to play by ear. The groups of four that he spoke of are apparently more

*I think that it is not that the tune does not "lend itself" to ornamentation. Instead, Bob Cheeseman never cared to or was not prepared, with his stock of formulas, to attempt more intricate ornamentation.

Buffalo Gals—version two

*In these two places, Bob dropped the last half of the measure. Bob Cheeseman is not accustomed to playing with other musicians, and there is no need to be "regular" when playing alone. For some fiddlers, irregularities may become part of a tune as they are repeated each time the tune is played. In that instance irregularities have musical significance. This irregularity seems to be the result of his getting lost or confused while ornamenting and not realizing the first measure is only half accounted for.

easily summoned forth if a player has not been restricted by a written score which discourages deviation. A fiddler who plays by ear becomes accustomed to varying his tunes. An "ear" player, exposed to ornamentation by other fiddlers, accepts variation. The more he hears it the more he notices both the circumstances under which it occurs and the ornaments that are employed. Gradually, he himself begins to embellish tunes.

As a fiddler myself, I first became aware of ornamentation on hearing Peter Schwimmer's "Turkey in the Straw." His version was much more elaborate than the melody I was familiar with. One afternoon Bob Doyle collected a version of "Turkey in the Straw" from Ralph Sauers. Ralph's version was simpler than Pete's. In fact it was quite similar to what I initially thought of when I first tried to play the tune. I think one can get an idea of how ornamentation works by examin-

Golden Slippers

ing and comparing these two versions. There can be no doubt that both versions are clearly recognizable as "Turkey in the Straw." However, going measure by measure, a difference between the versions appears in the first full bar. Version one has two eighth notes, both of which are G. On the other hand, version two replaces these eighth notes with four sixteenth notes: G, F sharp, G, and A. This four-note pattern unquestionably preserves the idea of the melody which was stated more simply in version one. In version two the G occurs at the same rhythmic interval but two additional tones are introduced which both lead from G and back to it. The second version effectively retains the tonality required for the passage while at the same time enlivening it by interspersing notes that lead immediately to or from the fundamental tones. Let us call the substitutive sequence of version two ornament A. The second part of the measure is identical in both versions.

The second entire measure is the same in both versions, but let us pause to examine whether or not both are ornamented. The first half of the measure is represented by a group of sixteenth notes which is little more than an inversion of

***Turkey in the Straw*—Ralph's version**

***Turkey in the Straw*—Pete's version**

ornament A. Rather than centering around G, this second "group of four" revolves around D. It is highly probable that both fiddlers replaced two eighth-note D's, the simplest statement of the melody, with an ornament which preserves D, yet enhances the passage, again by leading to and from the essential tone.

In measure 3 both fiddlers repeated the pattern of ornamentation they had used in measure 1. Here the essential tone is B. Version one simply uses two eighth-note B's to begin the measure where version two employs a group of four sixteenth notes—B, A, B, and C. This group is none other than ornament A, this time revolving around B. The second half of the measure is the same in both versions.

The fourth measure in each version is identical. Both employ a simple unornamented statement of the melody. Significant variation does not occur again until the eighth measure. While both versions resolve to the tonic using a quarter note, the approach to this repose is expressed differently in each. Version one very simply descends to G with two eighth notes, B and A. The second version employs a four-sixteenth-note cluster. The sequence begins on B, then jumps a fifth above the tonic to D. It then descends through B and A to G. The descent through B and A is intrinsic to the melody. Both versions effectively reach the tonic through these essential transitional tones; however, version two interjects a D. It fits easily because D is part of the G major scale and is a component of the major triad or basic chord of the tonic. The entire first beat of this last measure forms a transition to G, the tonic. Unlike ornament A, which was based on a different kind of melodic tone, this second ornament enlivens a transition. Let us dub this ornament B.

The only elements that differentiate these versions of "Turkey in the Straw" are ornaments A and B. If Ralph had these two ornaments at this command, and if he were accustomed to using them in the same melodic situation as Pete, both versions would be identical. Were Pete to have had additional ornaments, the versions might vary even more. The total stock of ornaments that a player has at his command will usually determine the variety of ornamentation in his tune versions. A player who is adept at responding to particular melodic circumstances with an assortment of substitutive formulas will frequently alter his renditions, where a fiddler with a limited supply of ornaments and an inability to recognize situations conducive to formulaic ornamentation will offer simpler tune versions.

When a fiddler learns a tune that already has been ornamented, he discovers "licks" he can use in other tunes. Being able to take note sequences from one tune and apply them to another is part of a player's ornamenting skill. This challenges a fiddler's imagination and often leads to innovative results.

One of the most common fiddle and banjo tunes is "Cripple Creek." Once David Bell played the extremely interesting rendition transcribed here. David was playing with the accompaniment of his brother-in-law, Clarence Bingaman, on the banjo. Normally, when playing with bluegrass musicians, each lead or melody-oriented instrument will alternate in taking solos or, in bluegrass language, "breaks." When David's turn came, he offered his rendition of the melody, which demonstrated very well his ability to apply ornaments he learned from tunes with flatted sevenths like "Old Joe Clark" to a tune which is almost always played with a major seventh. Throughout his solos, David consistently played a G natural rather than a G sharp, even when he descended to a lower octave. This flatted leading tone is the identifying element of the mixolydian mode used in a number of fiddle tunes such as "Old Joe Clark" and "Salt Creek." In the Buffalo Valley most mixolydian

Cripple Creek

fiddle tunes are in the key of A. I doubt whether it is a mere coincidence that "Cripple Creek" in this instance is also played in A. Familiar with flatted sevenths in the key of A, David found an innovative application for some of the ornaments he knew in the mixolydian mode by incorporating them into a traditionally Ionian melody.

The tunes in this book demonstrate that a fiddler's stock of ornaments need not be large to enable him to vary his tunes. Throughout David Bell's repertoire the same ornaments are used repeatedly. Even within a particular piece, a specific ornament may be employed over and over each time the melody permits its application. In the first line of David Bell's "Girl I Left behind Me," for example, parallel repetition occurs between entire measures. The first and second bars differ only in where the ornament begins. The ornamental sequence exemplified by the consecutive sixteenth notes E, F sharp, E, and D is not only repeated within "Girl I Left behind Me," but also throughout David's repertoire. Each fiddler discovers and develops ornaments which he finds easy to incorporate into his tune versions.

Though all fiddlers must be able to embellish their tunes to some degree, ornamentation is not the sole criterion on which an evaluation of a fiddler's proficiency should be based. Intonation, timing, and bowing techniques are all manifestations of a player's skill. A fiddler must play with ease, relaxed with his instrument. A player who can impart his own enjoyment of music to friends and neighbors provides a welcomed service to the community and deservedly earns the respect, admiration, and gratitude of all lovers of fiddle and dance music.

This chapter began by differentiating between fiddling and violin playing. Violin playing is a fine art; fiddling is a folk art. These two art forms differ in many ways, including the processes by which players learn their art. The learning process is complex for both art forms, but since violin playing is learned through more carefully defined procedures, it is easier to examine. While there are certain steps one must follow in order to learn to fiddle, a description of the steps can at best be only general. It is, after all, folk music, which the International Folk Music Council of 1954 defined as "the product of a musical tradition that has evolved through the process of oral transmission. The factors that shape the tradition are: (1) Continuity, which links the present with the past; (2) Variation, which springs from the individual; (3) Selection by the Community, which determines the form or forms in which the music survives." Although this does not account for all factors, it is a valuable starting point for our consideration of the learning process for fiddlers. What is it that inherently maintains these factors for them? How do continuity, variation, and selection preserve the coherency of the art, and at the same time permit its evolution?

Once a fiddler has an introductory knowledge of his instrument, he must isolate those qualities that specifically characterize the music he hopes to play. Fiddling has an identifiable "sound" that a beginner strives for. This "sound" is a manifestation of the art's continuity. It keeps fiddling recognizable through the years. Having discovered which techniques are necessary in order to achieve the desired "sound," a fiddler in effect has learned that which maintains the tradition.

Variation is bound to occur whenever people are the medium of transmission. Mistakes as well as creativity and originality all result in change. Ornamentation of a basic melody can mold a tune into a myriad of different shapes. If there is no objection by either audiences or other players, alterations of tunes will survive and possibly be passed on. Such efforts can eventually obscure basic tunes, but as long as the essential characteristics of the art are maintained, variation will be accepted or at least tolerated.*

The selection may be by the individual fiddler as well as the community. Ultimately, however, the community at large, through their influence on the fiddler's selection, will choose the innovations they wish to maintain and perpetuate. They will encourage continuation of what they like, and discourage what they do not like. Recently, bluegrass has brought major changes to the art of fiddling. Bluegrass has survived because it is generally accepted. Had Bill Monroe, the father of bluegrass, been laughed from the stage early in his music career, fiddlers still might not realize that their instruments can be played in the key of B. Instead, Monroe's bluegrass music did "catch on." At present, none of our middle-aged players who have been exposed to bluegrass have escaped its melodic and rhythmic influences.

When I first began to play the fiddle I worried that the art was dying. After all, I knew no one, nor had I ever known anyone, who played. As I focused more and more of my attention on fiddling, players began to appear. After five years as a band member and field researcher, I know fiddlers of a variety of ages and backgrounds. Though fiddling is not thriving like it did in years past, it seems to be attracting renewed interest. I can only hope that this interest continues, thus assuring the art's survival.

*See Samuel P. Bayard, "Two Representative Tune Families of British Tradition," *Midwest Folklore* 4, no. 1 (1954): 13–33.

4

Nonperforming Fiddlers: Bearers of the Tradition

Ralph Sauers and Archie Miller, along with Joe Bell, were once practiced fiddlers. They performed extensively throughout the Buffalo Valley. Now they have grown old, and only rarely play. Thus responsibility for maintaining the fiddling tradition in the valley for the most part has been relinquished to younger men. Each generation impresses on the fiddling tradition influences characteristic of its era. Regarding style and repertoire, Ralph and Archie did not bequeath to their children exactly what they themselves inherited. The nonperformers offer a unique look at fiddling as it was a few decades ago.

Ralph Sauers of Dice

Bob Doyle's father told him of a fiddler named Ralph Sauers who lived in the village of Dice near Mifflinburg. With good directions Bob found Ralph's place. So as not to be mistaken for a traveling salesman, he carried a fiddle by his side as he aproached the front door. Bob's knock drew a reluctant response. Anna Sauers had heard that a murderer was roaming the neighborhood, so she was understandably apprehensive about greeting strangers. After Bob explained the reason for his visit, however, the door was opened.

Ralph is the oldest living member of his extended family. All their lives the Sauers family have made the Buffalo Valley their home. Ralph was born and raised just a mile or two from where he now lives. He and Anna have four sons and four daughters, most of whom are married and have families of their own. Though the entire family has always loved Ralph's fiddling, only his son John has shown any interest in playing. He plays the guitar and mandolin and once tried fiddling but gave up because he could never seem to get the bowing.

Ralph Sauers poses with Bob's fiddle.

At first, Bob had a hard time getting Ralph to play or even answer questions. Before an interview could begin, Ralph insisted on showing Bob each fiddle in his collection. Many fiddlers are so infatuated with their instruments they love just looking at and fondling them. Ralph finally brought out his favorite, a viola strung with guitar and banjo strings so that it can be tuned to fiddle pitch. Ralph's "big fella," as he called it, was loud enough to be heard at square dances without amplification. Bob luckily had the tape recorder on.

Bob: When did you learn to play the fiddle?

Ralph: I was about 14 years old, and a neighbor boy who lived towards Mifflinburg played a guitar and a mandolin. He got me started on this mandolin, and eventually I switched to the fiddle.

Bob: Do you have that first one yet?

Ralph: No, I sold it. That was about 50 years ago, maybe a little longer, yeah, more than 50, I sold it. Oh, I don't remember the first fiddle or who owned it. I had so many. I had dozens of them in my time—all kinds. I'm gonna show you my fiddles.

Bob: Who gave you your first fiddle?

Ralph: No one ever gave me any. My parents never bothered me with anything unless I could get it myself, on my own. And I don't know who I got my first fiddle off of, but being able to play the mandolin, the keyboard is the same on the violin except there's no frets there, I could play the fiddle in a short time without any bother.

Bob: Do you remember what tunes you started learning the fiddle with?

Ralph: Well, the old-fashioned square dance pieces. The first tune I learned was "Home Sweet Home," about like everybody does—an easy one, and from there anything.

Bob: Do you remember what key that was in?

Ralph: G, always in G. And when I play by ear, it's that way yet. When I play by ear, most times I play in G, but now I can play in almost any key once I get started . . . I can play by note in the key of F, but by ear it don't go so good.

Anna: Pop didn't play by note, did he?

Ralph: Her father was an excellent violin player, one of the best you'd ever hear. He didn't know one note from another. He played all by ear; learned it all himself, he didn't play anything with frets.

Bob: I guess he was quite a square dance fiddler?

Ralph Sauer's father-in-law, Horace Zimmerman, and his wife. Horace could call and play for a square dance at the same time.

Ralph: Oh, my yes! That's all he done, one of the best, and he could call too. He could call off and play at the same time, he was an expert at that.* You see, they'd get about half chiggered sometimes, and get pretty handy at the square dances to get the fiddle bow under the ladies' skirts. That'll make 'em jump! Oh yes, he was tricky, and a comical old fellow. You'd kill yourself laughing at him. He'd take a little mouth organ about so long so you couldn't see it and play on that thing, and do it all with his tongue, the darn little thing. Yeah, he was good in music. And now we're gonna get down to them fiddles!

*Calling and playing for a square dance is very difficult. Joe Bell mentioned that his father could call and play at the same time. We have yet to encounter a fiddler with such a talent.

Bob: OK, I'll put mine into tune too.

Ralph: You know, I've no place to keep my fiddles, so I stole some of her cupboard room.

Anna: He has no place to keep nothin'.

Ralph: I wish I had my third fiddle here; it's genuine Italian cause it's burnt right on the back of the wood. Now this one here ain't no violin, and I'll tell you what it was got for. This is a viola; it's bigger than a fiddle! This friend of mine, the fella [Cleve Aumiller] who organized the string band in Mifflinburg, he was a good fiddle player, and didn't know one note from the other. And at that time they had no amplifiers for fiddles, and he played for square dances, and his fiddle didn't have the volume he wanted, so he got this viola from I don't know who. And the reason he strung it is that a violin string is too short so he took banjo and guitar strings, and that's what's on it. He tuned it like a fiddle and had a whole lot more volume than a regular fiddle for square dances. Me and him were good friends all his life, and when he got so old that he didn't play any more, I asked him one day, "What will you take for this outfit?" "Bein' 'tis you," he said, "I paid fifteen dollars for it, and you can have it fer that." I'll tell you I jumped for it mighty fast.

Intermittently, Ralph played with Cleve Aumiller's Mifflinburg String Band, which was originally formed in 1912. Enjoying great popularity, the band traveled throughout central Pennsylvania playing for parades, dances, and concerts. Ralph remembered they used to travel in an old Buick truck. Since the band had fifteen to twenty members, it was a tight fit with all the instruments and musicians. "This is happy time for me, to spend this time," Ralph explained as he reminisced.

Since Aumiller's string band was so large, its members often got together in smaller groups to form bands of their own or just to play informally. All the musicians in the area had a way of gravitating toward one another. Ralph used to carry his fiddle everywhere. He constantly found or started sessions with others who shared his love of music. These opportunities offered the chance for everyone to learn new tunes and "licks."

The weekend square dance was by far the biggest local attraction. Playing for it was so prestigious that it inspired many young people to try to learn an instrument. A younger player was always welcome on stage among the older musicians. If the band called a number which their new member did not know, he just played along as well as he could. By the end of the dance he had usually learned the tune. Fiddlers rarely forget the first time they played in public.

Bob: How long did it take you from the time you started playing to the first time you ever played in public?

Ralph: Well, that's too long ago. I wouldn't know what to tell you. Then, really, the first time I played in public that amounted to anything a whole lot was I got to play for a square dance in Centerville [now called Penns Creek].

Bob: When was that? Do you remember?

Ralph: Oh my God, I was about sixteen years old, probably. Cleve Aumiller organized a string band here in Mifflinburg and us young fellas around here got very interested in music and stuff, of course, and so I don't know how many of us there was, but I guess, as near as I can tell you, it was the first string band in Pennsylvania, and maybe in the United States, all I know. I played with them several years, and from there wherever I went, I always had an instrument with me of some kind.

Bob: Did you go into the Army?

Ralph: No, I missed all that by three weeks. I wanted to enlist when my brothers left, but I was too young, and my parents wouldn't sign [me] off, so that left me back. I had my examination and was waiting for the call card to go to camp, but it [World War I] broke up before I got called, and that was the end of it. And after that, I don't know, it just seems that I was lucky enough that I missed every one after that. I was born in the year of the Spanish-American War, 1898, but I never got in any battles.

Bob: Let's talk about the violin now.

Ralph: Of course I played like a young fella because when you roam around, wherever you sat, anyone around you played music.*

Ralph: And that's the way it was, here and there, all over. I worked over in lumber camp, over in Juniata [Centre County, Pennsylvania]. I even had my fiddle over there and I played there in the lumber camp. Yeah, I played wherever I went. I always had an instrument with me. Then I played for square dances, and wherever they danced and with different people. And then, my eldest son, John over there, I bought him a guitar. He was young, and, like us, eventually he learned to play it by playing around here with the neighbor boys, and now he has a band of his own. I played in that [band] for a couple of years, down

*Ralph suggests that when he was young there were many more musicians than today. Harry Daddario agrees that when he was a boy, older fiddlers, guitar players, etc., were seemingly everywhere.

there at Kratzerville, and for clambakes . . . anything that came up. I knowed they had a carnival here from time to time, and they was having a bunch of young dancers come from down the country somewhere, and they had their own players, but evidently their players didn't come. But the dancers were there. Then they had no one to play for them at this carnival. We were on the grounds, and they hollered us up, got us together, and we furnished the music. When this thing ended, the head guy of this outfit come up to us and said, "I'm glad our musicians didn't come; you had better music than our outfit could ever furnish." That's what he told us.

Bob: When you were playing square dances, what were the dances that were popular? What did people dance to, and what were the tunes you liked to play for them?

Ralph: Well, I played a lot of them pieces. I didn't know the name of them. I just learned them from the other fellas I played with. I had an awful good memory. If I'd hear a piece one time, at that time I knowed it already. And a lot of 'em I played I didn't know the name, but all of them clear old pieces.

Bob: Do you remember the name of the dances?

Ralph: Well, I don't know the calls what they called. I was actually that interested in music I paid no attention to the calls. I was interested in the music that we furnished. All them old fashioned pieces, "Golden Slippers," and what. All that old stuff, that's real old now, and it's comin' back.* . . . I worked out in Kansas on my way west, I and my buddy. We shocked wheat in Kansas. The place we stayed by good luck was an uncle of my buddy. He [the uncle] played the piano and had a fiddle. He used to set evenings and play the piano, you know. He had his head back, and had a little goatee. It used to amuse me to watch him. I seen his fiddle settin', but I didn't say nothing for a while. Then one evening I said to him, "Is something in that fiddle box?" I got it out, tuned it up, and was ready to go. He started playin', and I knowed a lot of the pieces he played. I played with him right away, and my God, I couldn't get away from him after that hardly. When we left there, he gave my buddy a twenty dollar bill, and he gave me the same thing. He gave us each a twenty dollar bill and made a farewell party for us.

*Old is certainly a relative term to Ralph and the other players. Any tune popular when they were young or when their fathers were young is considered old. Many pieces in the fiddler's repertoire can be traced to popular song airs only a few decades old. Other tunes have histories which stretch over centuries.

Bob: Could you continue about the square dances and the square dance playing?

Ralph: I just heard them like I told ya. I'd play with a fiddle player, and every here and there was an old fiddle player that still played square dances. I was a younger fellow, and they'd ask me to set in and play with them and help play for the square dance. An naturally I learned the pieces.

Bob: Besides learning the pieces, did you learn the way they played too?

Ralph: Well, I guess I did to a certain extent.

Bob: Did you ever play bluegrass music?

Ralph: Any what?

Bob: Any bluegrass with a bluegrass band?

Ralph: Not that I know of.

Bob: Do you remember some people saying that the devil teaches a fiddler how to play? Did you ever hear that the fiddle was the devil's instrument?

Ralph: I believe I heard that mentioned. That was on account of square dancing and what happens at square dances, you know what I mean.

Bob: No, explain.

Ralph: Well, you know what happens at a lot of square dances when there's a bunch of young people and married people. They either change with each other, and then there's trouble and stuff. You know what I mean. One fellow might pick up the other fellow's woman when he's talking and walk out the door. I just heard that the devil was in your fiddle because they played them at square dances. And you know what can happen at a square dance. A lot of trouble always come from them square dance parties. Family trouble! I didn't go for that stuff.

[They began playing later in the interview.]

Ralph: I might play a little bit of it [a tune he titled "The Virginia Reel"]. Oh, if I play a week or two again, you'd find a big difference out when you'd hear me play.*

Bob: Well, we'll be back so. . . .

*"The Virginia Reel," a tune as well as a dance, is the title by which Ralph knew the piece. Its common American title is "Old Molly Hare," akin to the European "Fairy Dance" or "Fairy Reel." A contra dance and not a square dance per se, the Virginia Reel dance, as it is commonly called in the United States, is derived from an English dance, "Sir Roger deCoverly," which was danced to a 9/8 time jig. For further information refer to William Chappell, *Popular Music of the Olden Time* (rpt. New York: Dover, 1965), p. 535.

Ralph: I used to be at one time, was supposed to be the best fiddle player around here at one time.

Bob: But you don't do badly, not at all.

Ralph: Yeah, but I hear all my mistakes, all my flaws on it. . . . Now my old stumpy finger don't get into place, and its's so hard for me to get out of first position. [Ralph lost part of his left index finger in an accident.]

Ralph was severely out of practice, but undaunted, he attempted tune after tune. The years had taken their toll. From the tapes of the interviews, however, I was able to extract transcriptions of three pieces: "Merry Maiden Polka," "Turkey in the Straw," and "Yankee Doodle." Ralph played these tunes very simply, although he probably had played them much more elaborately in his prime.

Ralph kept a handwritten collection of many tunes he used to play. He picked up most of his square dance tunes by ear, but so that he could play some of the popular pieces of his day, he learned to read music. He still has the tattered texts of the correspondence course which urged him to practice his bowing and fingering

Merry Maiden Polka

Turkey in the Straw

Yankee Doodle

in order to remove the "scratchy tone" from his playing. Examples from his written collection show the diversity of his musical interests.

These examples form only a small part of Ralph's total repertoire. During the interviews Ralph played part or all of the following pieces (Ralph's titles):

Turkey in the Straw	Maple on the Hill
Irish Washerwoman	Virginia Reel
Merry Maiden Polka	Rock 'n Rye Polka
Yankee Doodle	Arkansas Traveller
Johnson's Rag	Little Indians
Girl I Left behind Me	Golden Slippers
Mockingbird Hill	Oh Mother It Hurts Me So
The Kingdom	Grey Eagle Hornpipe
Marching through Georgia	Rickett's Hornpipe

Additionally, he kept the music for the other tunes he used to play:

Leather Breeches	When They Play the Polka
Wasoly Kominiarczyk	White Silver Sands
Alabama Jubilee	Firefly Waltz
Mack's Rag	Fräulein
Twelfth Street Rag	Sugar Time
Tiger Rag	Apple Blossom Time
Five Foot Two	Cuckoo Waltz
In the Middle of an Island	Blue Shirt Waltz
Lichtensteiner Polka	Bummer's Reel
Barbara Polka	Hawaiian Sunset
Bright Red Horizon	Clarinet Polka

One might, for good reason, wonder what "Five Foot Two" and "Tiger Rag" are doing alongside "Arkansas Traveller" and "Grey Eagle" in the repertoire of a traditional fiddler. Let's consider the influences that may have inspired Ralph to learn such pieces.

Although economic disaster struck many during the Great Depression, musicians enjoyed an enviable demand for their talents. "In 1932, when beer came back," Archie Miller explained, "every saloon wanted a band." But they wanted more than a square dance band. The customers insisted that the musicians play popular contemporary pieces. Fiddlers like Ralph Sauers had to learn tunes like "Tiger

Gray Eagle Hornpipe

Leather Breeches

*Fire Fly Waltz**

*Peculiarities in Ralph's handwritten version suggest he did not follow the sheet music very closely. I have retained the version exactly as it was written.

Rag," "Five Foot Two," and "Alabama Jubilee." Since these numbers were not known or played by those from whom Ralph usually learned tunes, he decided to learn to read music. Through sheet music he was then able to add popular music to his repertoire. These modern pieces did not replace but merely supplemented those traditional tunes which he continued to play at square dances.

Forming bands to play at bars brought together the most unlikely combinations of instruments. A fiddler occasionally found himself sandwiched among accordions, saxophones, pianos, or Hawaiian guitars, playing in keys he hardly knew existed. In these situations the fiddler was often forced to accommodate those instruments in the band which commonly rendered tunes in flat keys. The traditional fiddler, accustomed to playing in G, D, A, and C, found himself in a bind. Some fiddlers just "faked it," but others—Joe Bell, Ralph Sauers, and Archie Miller—claim they coped with the problem by learning to read music and thereby acquiring fluency in most keys. How well any of these players could actually read we cannot accurately determine since they no longer play. I suspect, however, that their reading ability was not developed to the extent it is remembered to have been.

While Ralph was an active player, popular songs, ragtime pieces, and other tunes sifted into his traditional repertoire. The burgeoning recording industry exposed the public to a great variety of music, thus expanding the tastes and ultimately the demands of Ralph's listening and dancing audiences. The modern pieces he learned were maintained side by side with the traditional ones. They received unbiased acceptance. Ralph's traditonal numbers, while basic to his repertoire, were not important to him solely because they were traditional. He did not see his role as being a bearer of folk tradition bound exclusively to maintaining authorless melodies. To him, the oldtime square dance tunes were just that, square dance tunes. Ralph found nothing inconsistent with being a traditional player and at the same time learning to read music so that he could play popular music.

When Ralph, Archie, and Joe passed their tradition to the next generation, they had no way of predicting which tunes would survive and which would not. That determination was up to the new players. Although the changing tastes of the community would surely influence the repertoires of each succeeding generation, many tunes were bound to be kept. Looking at the tunes we collected from our active players, one sees that indeed many have been retained. While most of the popular period pieces have not weathered transmission, many of the traditional tunes have. "Arkansas Traveller," "Flop-Eared Mule," "Turkey in the Straw," and "The Girl I Left behind Me" seem to be known by every fiddler in the Buffalo Valley, young and old.

The coherence of the art is fundamentally tied to the traditional tunes. They embody the rhythms, cadences, lilts, and melodic contours which define fiddling. Through these tunes the art is transmitted, almost intact, from generation to generation. It is essential that the traditional airs survive. Tunes which merely represent the expressions of current tastes are not basic to tradition even though they may influence it. They can therefore fade with the generation to whom they belong without jeopardizing the continuance of the art.

The picture Ralph painted of fiddling, as it was when he was learning, and as it became in his active years, helped us understand and appreciate the transmission and evolutionary processes. Ralph was by far the most colorful and enthusiastic of our nonperforming players. It will be a long time before his stories slip from my memory.

Archie Miller of Lewisburg

Bob and I were visiting David and Laura Bell one afternoon when Archie Miller, who lives across the road, stopped by. At the age of seventy-eight Archie married his second wife, Belle Bingaman, Laura's mother. Few would have guessed from looking at Archie that he was eighty-one years old. His appearance more suggested a man of sixty. We explained to Archie the nature of our project and asked him if he would be available for an interview. He invited us to stop by but warned that he no longer played.

We finally found Archie at home. The weather was beautiful, and happily Archie was in a cooperative and congenial mood. He was extremely shy about playing for us, but we managed to coax him into fiddling a few tunes. From the way he held his instrument and his bow we could tell that his skill had once been considerable, but on that day Archie was severely out of practice from years of inactivity. Like Ralph Sauers and Joe Bell, Archie kept a handwritten collection of tunes which he allowed us to copy. Using the titles he attributed to each tune, we listed all the pieces he either attempted to play or had written out.

The Kingdom
Old Kingdom (Harry's "Sweet 16")
Old 97
Red River Valley
Old Lauderbach
Redwing
Mississippi Sawyer
99 Years
Missouri Waltz
The Waltz You Saved for Me
The Butcher's Boy
21 Years
Loch Lomond
Captain Jinks
Banjo's Silent Now

When he was active, Archie often played a number of popular period pieces. Like Ralph he maintained them in his repertoire along with the tunes he played for square dances. Archie learned to read music, as did many of his contemporaries, so that he could satisfy both his own musical interests and the demands of his audiences.

We once learned from Harry Daddario that Archie had won the Bucknell University Folk Festival Fiddle Competition in 1936. During one of our interviews we asked Archie about the contest.

Matthew: Did you enter a lot of contests?

Archie: There was only one contest, in 1936, but we were traveling around playing square dances and things like that, and conceived the idea we'd win the contest.

Matthew: How many tunes did you have to play?

Archie: Only one! There was a row of benches there, and about seven or eight fiddlers. I was sitting out on the end—the last one.

Matthew: What did the other people play?

Archie: Oh, jigs and reels and things like that. You know, each fiddler is different.

Bob: Please tell us more about the convention.

Archie: Well, I didn't expect to win it. We were packed and ready to leave when they called my name.

Matthew: Were some pretty good fiddlers there?

Archie: Some pretty good fiddlers there? Oh yeah!

Matthew: Did you know any of them?

Archie: No. They came from the coal regions, and I was the only one from around this territory that entered.

Matthew: Is that the only contest you ever entered?

Archie: Yes.

(The following three tunes were copied from Archie's hand-written collection.)

Red River Valley

Captain Jinx

Matthew: So, you won every one you ever entered?
Bob: That's a 100% record. Pretty good I'd say.*

*The fiddle competition, Archie informed us, included a square dance band contest, but their caller, Elmer Krick, got drunk, and Archie's band could not enter.

*The Missouri Waltz**

*This tune is obviously in G even though, in the hand-written collection, the key signature indicates C. A few of the accidentals seem to be missing as well.

During the interview Archie asked one of us to play a tune, so I played a piece which I had learned from Harry Daddario, "The Kingdom." Smiling, Archie told us that "The Kingdom" was taken from an old song he knew. We prodded him into singing as much as he could remember.

Kingdom Comin' *

1. Oh, have you seen the master with a moustache on his face?
   He was on the road this morning trying to leave this place.
   (Refrain)
   The massa run ha-ha-ha-ha, and the darkies say ho-ho.
   It must be now in the Kingdom Comin' in the Year of Jubilee.
2. He's six-foot-one and weighed two for the other and weighed three hundred pounds.
   His coat's so big it wouldn't fit him; it go half way around.
   Refrain.
3. They locked him up in the smokehouse; threw the keys down in the well.
   He's old enough, big enough, ought to know better; couldn't wait a spell.
   Refrain.

We had only two visits with Archie, and because he was so out of practice, he was extremely reluctant to play for us. We once witnessed the rare occurrence of his playing in public during the New Berlin Annual July 4 parade in 1975. Riding on a float with several other musicians, he turned as Bob photographed him and quipped, "Well, you finally heard me play!"

With the nonperforming players in the Buffalo Valley we were able to see continuity and changes in fiddling through three generations. Ralph Sauers, Archie Miller, and Joe Bell not only explained what fiddling was like when they were active players, but they also described the tradition as they inherited it from their forefathers. Horace Zimmerman, Ralph Sauers' father-in-law, Archie Miller's dad, from whom Archie learned to play, and Joe Bell's father, Henry E. Bell, all played exclusively by ear. They also restricted their repertoires almost entirely to dance

*Archie's title "Kingdom Comin' " is also commonly known as "The Kingdom," or "The Year of Jubilee(o)."

Archie Miller at the Fourth of July parade.

tunes. Horace and Henry had the amazing ability to fiddle and call a square dance at the same time, a talent that is now totally extinct in the valley.

Now that Ralph and his contemporaries no longer actively bear the tradition, it has been taken up by the next generation, the David Bells and Marvin Kratzers. Each generation is influenced simultaneously by forces which maintain tradition and by forces which vary that tradition. Learning to read music and playing popular commercial tunes were the primary peculiarities of Ralph's and Archie's generation. Their successors are exploring bluegrass-style fiddling in addition to playing the oldtime square dance tunes. How long bluegrass will continue to attract fiddlers can only be determined by future generations and the audiences for whom they perform.

5

The Square Dance Fiddler: Building a Partnership with the Caller

There are several types of fiddling. Nowadays, the two most common are bluegrass and oldtime, or square dance, style. Taking a close look at both these kinds of playing was one of Bob's and my purposes.

A good oldtime fiddler can, to quote an old saying, "make a cow dance." There is a vibrancy and vitality to square dance playing which to many is synonymous with fiddling itself. Harry Daddario, one of the best oldtime players we encountered, is the focus of our study of oldtime playing. In addition to providing a glimpse of Harry's personality through our interviews with him, this chapter will offer a fairly detailed look at some of the techniques used by oldtime fiddlers, and it will discuss why they play almost exclusively in the keys of G, D, A, and C.

Oldtime playing, for the most part, is square dance playing. At a square dance, the fiddler, his accompanying musicians, the caller, and the dancers must work in harmony. To coordinate the interaction, the fiddler must be sensitive to the needs of all. Harry's awareness of this responsibility was one more reason we chose him to exemplify the oldtime fiddler.

We learned about Harry Daddario from Joe Bell. Joe thought that Harry still played for square dances. Bob and I had yet to interview a fiddler who was an active player so we stopped by to see Harry. We knocked at his door and soon a stirring from within produced a curious, friendly middle-aged man.

Bob immediately stepped forward and explained the reason for our visit. We were hoping to talk about fiddling and maybe even play a few tunes. Unhappily, Harry told us that he and his wife were about to go for a ride and that he could only offer us a "rain check." We were clearly disappointed and turned to leave when Harry had a change of heart. He asked us to wait a minute while he found out from his wife, Evelyn, whether he had time for a few tunes while she was getting ready. Harry soon returned and invited us in.

After introductions we got out our instruments. Harry fiddled while we played backtime. The time slipped by quickly as we moved from tune to tune. Eventually Harry laid down his fiddle and went to see what was keeping Evelyn. By this time Evelyn had been waiting for about an hour and a half; her patience with Harry's fiddling had worn extremely thin. Aware of our imposition, Bob and I were soon on our way with an invitation to return when we could spend a little more time.

Bob and I visited Harry often. Our relationship with him grew relaxed and comfortable. As a fledgling fiddler, I sought technical advice and at the same time hoped to learn some tunes that I could play for square dances. I used to tape each interview and later, at home, transcribe the tunes Harry had played. During subsequent interviews, Harry and I would play the tunes I had learned. Two of the first were "Bummer's Reel" and "Goodbye Old Rover."

Harry enjoyed being a teacher. He went over tunes very slowly so that I could scratch about and find the right notes. He seemed to think I could learn tunes instantly and insisted that we try pieces I had no hope of being able to play. Offering advice, he often drew attention to shortcomings in my technique.

Harry: May I correct you something?
Matthew: Sure.
Harry [Pointing to the section of the strings closer to the bridge than to the end of the fingerboard]: Play here! You play over here. You can get a better tone right across here.

I appreciated Harry's concern. The command he had over his instrument gave him authority in my eyes. Harry had gone beyond just learning to play his instrument. Once Harry mentioned he had done some trick fiddling in his younger days. We were eager to find out what kind of tricks he did. It took a little prodding, but Harry finally went along with our request.

Photo courtesy Penn State Information Service

Harry fiddles a tune on his front porch.

Matthew: Joe [Dietrich] told me you did some trick fiddling for him.
Bob: Oh, yes.
Matthew: I wondered if you could play. . . .
Bob: Come on, Harry, it sure was neat. We told on you.
Harry: I used to do the, ah, back here, but I couldn't never do it again. I get tangled up. [Holding the fiddle behind his neck, he played a phrase of a tune.] No, I can't do that.
Bob: How about, you did it behind your back. [Harry put the fiddle behind his back.] There it is.
Matthew: I keep telling these guys I'm going to learn to do a little of that.
Harry: Well, I can't, you ought to have your violin, you know, back in your back, see, my arms supposed to be like this, see, you oughtn't to be looking at what you're doing, you know, you oughtn't be doing it while looking.

Bob: Just standing there smiling.
Harry: Sure, I got something up here, if it still goes there.
Bob: OK, here he goes.
Matthew: I can't do it. I can't get my arm socket back there.
Harry: You have to practice. You can't do things right away; it takes time. Then we used to do this, play like this. [Holding the bow with his knees, he rubbed the fiddle against the bow.]
Bob: With the bow between your knees?
Harry: I used to play a lot of tunes like this, gosh yes. I'd do all kinds of stuff.
Bob: While you were standing up, or did you sit down?
Harry: Oh, you have to sit down.
Bob: Here, well, sit down.
Harry: No, no, no, I can't do it anyhow; I just wanted to show [you how I used to do it]. We used to do a lot, then one fella'd be bowing my fiddle like this. The other guy'd hold it, and I'd be bowing your fiddle, and you'd be bowing mine.
Matthew: Both together?
Harry: Yeah, we done that, sure.
Matthew: Like this, you would be bowing this one and I'd be bowing that one?
Harry: Yeah, yeah, we did that. The first one we'd start, one fella'd stand here and finger and you'd be bowing it, see, you'd take the bow and then. . . .
Bob: Why don't you try it? Go ahead, just for fun.
Harry: Oh, no, I can't do that.
Matthew: I can't do that.
Bob: You don't think so?
Matthew: That takes a lot of work.
Harry: That takes time.

Trick fiddling was only a temporary comic diversion. We soon moved on.

Harry's experience with the fiddle encompasses its repair as well as its playing. Understanding the care a fiddle requires in order that its tone be maintained, Harry suggested I wipe off the rosin which had accumulated on my fiddle.

Matthew: You know how you see fiddlers with rosin all over the fiddle?
Harry: Well, I keep it wiped off.
Matthew: Keep it wiped off, you think?
Harry: Yeah, that's the craziest thing you'd ever in God's life heard of. Some of

those cracks [crackpots] think it will make a better sound. It kills the sound. Keep it off there.

Matthew: I try to keep it wiped off, but I use a lot of rosin.

Harry: Keep wiping it off. Don't leave it get on there, cause that'll cake up and cake up, and after a while it will kill the sound of your violin. Them old guys had some weird ideas. Crazy.

Bob: What were some of the other weird ideas?

Harry: Well, they wouldn't have a chin rest. They say it will kill the tone. That's crazy, too. There's nothing to that. I have one violin soaked clear through [from perspiration]. The old guys playing it clear through the wood, couldn't ever get it off. It stained clear through.

Harry's devotion to the fiddle cannot even be fully expressed by his ability to both play and repair it. Fiddles and fiddling are a total preoccupation. Each instrument has a personality and disposition. Maintaining an extensive collection of fiddles, Harry often took time to show us various shapes, qualities, and styles.

Initially, Bob's working relationship with Harry differed in one important respect from mine. I approached Harry as a student. I wanted to learn to fiddle both for personal enjoyment and so that I might develop a subjective approach for our study of fiddlers and fiddling. Bob's concern focused more on Harry as a tradition-bearer. Bob diligently recorded the biographical and other data which he thought were essential. Harry's cooperation with both Bob's and my aspects of the collecting project grew from a respect for our purpose and a pride in his art. He loved being an authority. When he found we were interested in the history of traditional square dance pieces, he was quick to offer an account of how "Soldier's Joy" got its name.

Harry: Oh, "The Kingdom," that's from the Civil War, you know. Same as "Soldier's Joy." You know that's how that came about. When they had that surrender and peace, the soldiers were so happy that they played "Soldier's Joy." *

Bob: Is that how it came from a dance to a march tune?

Harry: Sure, sure.

*In fact the melody usually associated with "Soldier's Joy" goes back much further than the Civil War. Harry's explanation of the tune's history is charming nonetheless.

Bob: I mean a march to a dance?

Harry: Right, right, right, sure.

Bob: Well, were these tunes marches during the Civil War?

Harry: Well, they weren't to be marched. They were just, ah, it was a joy for the soldiers. It was a celebration like a, what would you call it? You know, a peace treaty. They were so happy, and they played that for the soldiers' joy. And that's how it got its name, "The Soldier's Joy."

I was surprised to learn Harry was in his sixties when we first met. He seemed so much younger. Fiddling must have rejuvenated him. Hardly being able to recall when he was not infatuated with fiddles and fiddling, Harry has been playing since he was a boy. We asked Harry where he learned most of his tunes.

Harry: Calvin Walters, he learned me all these tunes. I was just, oh I don't know, five years old, six, when I used to play these tunes.

Bob: Where was this?

Harry: Well, it was right over here in Snyder County. They'd have these square dances out at our neighbor's, the Reese's, and they would square dance every week. We could go there and, ah.

Bob: How did your parents take to your playing music?

Harry: Well, I'd just sit there, you know, I was well behaved. I'd just sit there by the fiddler, and was there all night sitting by that old man.

Bob: You and your brother?

Harry? Yeah, well, my brother, he'd more tear around and devil me all the time, you know. He'd be playing with the other kids, the kids would be there by themselves. I'd be by the old man Walters. I'd just sit there around beside of him all night long.

Bob: Is that right?

Harry? I believe I used to say, "Mr. Walters, I wish I could play a violin." He'd say, "Well, cheer up, Harry [someday you will be able to]." I just loved the violin, you know.

Calvin Walters' prediction came true; Harry became quite a fiddler. From the beginning it was dance fiddling which most attracted him and exerted the greatest influence on him. The weekly hoedown provided the inspiration to learn, the exposure to fundamental tunes and techniques, and eventually even the audience for whom he could display his talent. Older men who played for the dances, like

Calvin Walters, offered assistance and served as models upon which Harry could pattern his playing. Like the fiddling of the older men from whom he learned, Harry's playing is strong and rhythmic. From his description of the older players, it appears he adopted their style, techniques, and even posture.

Harry grasps the fiddle in his left hand with the neck resting in his palm. He holds the bow well above the frog and keeps his wrist fairly straight during the bowing motion. Most string changes are made with his wrist and elbow, only later bringing his shoulder into line. Technically, this stance might appall a classical player, yet it allows Harry all the freedom he needs to play the way he wants to. Harry's playing is rhythmically very dynamic. While his ornamentation is neither elaborate nor demanding, he imparts to his tunes an undeniable vivacity.

Over the years, fiddling has had to respond to a number of demands or requirements. For a square dance, the fiddle has to be loud, rhythmic, and melodically simple. In order to satisfy these requisites, dance fiddling naturally had to develop certain techniques.

First, the fiddle has had to overcome one overpowering obstacle: the noise created by a barn full of dancing people. When Harry was young, the fiddler could not rely on a microphone to augment his volume. Without electronic amplification, it is essential that the fiddle be played as loudly and as rhythmically as possible. The rustle of countless shoes across a dance floor creates such a racket that a fiddler and his accompanying musicians often have quite a job just being heard. I once played a square dance where only the caller had a microphone. The band was having such a difficult time following the tunes, I could hardly believe that the dancers were able to hear the music. When I asked a few of them, everyone affirmed that the band, especially the fiddle, needed to be louder. Though audibility continued to be a problem, the dancers and the band managed to follow the tunes as long as I played loudly and rhythmically. It was not necessary that the tunes be masterfully performed, only that they be rhythmically distinct and loud enough to be heard.

Since two vibrating strings create more sound than only one, one way to enhance the volume of a fiddle is to bow two strings at the same time. This technique usually requires that only one string be fingered. The second string can be used as a drone. Often, however, a player does finger both strings, or double stop, in which case he most frequently employs thirds and fifths as harmonic intervals.

There is another volume-enhancing technique which involves the use of two strings and makes it possible either to drone the tonic or to play it on two strings simultaneously. By stopping a string with the fourth finger at the position which results in the same tone as the next higher open string, the tonic can be either doubled or droned while a melody is fingered on the string which in the open position usually provides the tonic. All these drones and double stops help to make the fiddle louder.

Another obvious way to increase the volume is for the fiddler to use more pressure on the bow. Most dance fiddlers play with a very heavy bow stroke. Though bowing this way can cause one's playing to sound "scratchy" unless accompanied by mellowing left- and right-hand techniques, it is not objectionable in noise-filled dance halls. A heavy bow stroke also helps create a clear rhythm which cuts through peripheral noise.

The need for intense rhythm is at least as important as the need for maximum volume. Certainly a tune must be audible, but its rhythm must also be monotonously relentless. Rhythm helps to lead the dancers and it holds together the accompanying musicians. To enhance a tune's rhythmic or danceable qualities, bowing styles have developed which strongly accentuate the beat. Each time a note is bowed rather than slurred, there is a punctuation. Also, the intensity with which each note is bowed allows for a slight variation in punctuation among the notes. A repeating pattern of bow strokes will create a recurring rhythmic sequence. Since any of a variety of bowing patterns can yield rhythmic patterns appropriate for accompanying various dances, many styles have developed within the broad spectrum of Anglo-American fiddling.

Bearing down heavily, Harry likes to bow almost every note in his tunes. This is not uncommon among the square dance fiddlers in the Buffalo Valley, and among some of the younger, more bluegrass-oriented fiddlers whose playing is a product of indirect dance influence. Harry may occasionally bow more than one note with one stroke, but he usually confines such slurring to waltzes. In a waltz, the first beat of the rhythmic triad dominates each measure and hence must be bowed. Because the emphasis is so heavily on the initial beat, the second two can be slurred without the cadence being weakened or sacrificed. Ignoring waltzes, let us reiterate that rhythmic bowing of oldtime fiddling, combined with droning and double stopping, has produced a clearly identifiable square dance style.

Even though the dance has in many ways forced a fiddling style, it has become reciprocally dependent on that style in order to maintain proper spirit, mood, and cadence. Dennis Ricker is a caller with whom I have often worked. In one of our

interviews with Dennis, he explained how the caller and the band interact, and he described the style of fiddling which has become so married to square dancing.

Dennis: Well, the best bands to work with are those that you don't have to say anything to except wave your arms to start up. "Fire in the Hole!" Out there [in Indiana] the caller is almost a part of the music. I mean he doesn't sing, but the music and the chant—they do kind of an auctioneer's kind of thing. For the country square dance you have to have the right kind of tune. There's a country hoedown sound that comes from a double-stopped fiddle that you just cannot duplicate; that makes up good oldtime square dancing. The thing about it is that the tune has to be relatively simple and have a very definite beat. You cannot square dance to a lot of bluegrass tunes. First of all, they are often too fast, and you have to have a very definite beat. Things like "Boil Them Cabbages Down," or "Ragtime Annie," I think is one of the best; it has the best sound. It keeps a good solid beat there, not too much embellishment. You've got to have the whole band in there all the time because the audience has to hear that music all the time to set the pace. The band's caller likes a certain rhythm, and the dancers are pretty comfortable with it, and that rhythm has to be pretty steady. The beat shouldn't be lost! Now I'm talking from my own experience, from a midwestern background. There are not many singing calls.

Bob: Let's discuss the music relative to the calling. Your instrumentation would be the banjo, bass, guitar. Your lead instrument would be the fiddle. From the caller's point of view, you would prefer the fiddle not to play a lot of licks or a lot of single-string playing; a lot of shuffling.

Dennis: Right! A lot of shuffling, double stopping, doubling—you get that drone sound—that hoedown sound.

Dennis pointed to those qualities which he thinks are characteristic of square dance fiddling. Working in conjunction with the caller who directs the dance, the fiddler must provide a strong lead for the dancers, the caller, and the rest of the band. Once, while playing "The Kingdom" for a square dance, this responsibility became painfully apparent to me. I started the dance by playing the simple version, which I had learned from Harry, and then I gradually incorporated ornamentation into the tune. The more I ornamented the less functional my playing became. The caller and the dancers began to lose cohesiveness as ornamentation engulfed my rhythm. It got so bad that the rest of the band could hardly follow me. As you notice by the slurs, I was bowing far fewer notes in the ornamented version than in the simple one. The beat became less and less prominent as I more and more sacrificed rhythm for ornamentation. I finally realized, as the dance continued to deteriorate, that I had better return to the simple rhythmic version and save the "fancy" rendition for a suitable situation. Since then I have always tried to remember that the job of the square dance fiddler is to maintain a loud rhythmic lead.

From the dancer's point of view, intricate ornamentation goes largely unnoticed. The dancers are preoccupied with the directions of the caller. Mike Lake, a friend of mine from Old Fort, Pennsylvania, has been a square dancer for years. We asked what the dancers expect from the musicians.

The Kingdom—Harry's version

The Kingdom—my ornamentation

Mike: This gets insulting, but the band is just there to support the caller, and I think good bands just follow the caller—the right tempo and the right noise level to complement him so that the dancers can keep the beat. And there *is* a definite beat to a square dance. The music makes the whole square dance. You can't have a square dance without a band, but the band is the thing that nobody notices. They pay attention to the caller.

Bob: You only notice it [the band] when it stops.

Mike: Yeah, and when you get out of step!

Bob: One step further—the relationship of the band to the caller.

Mike: You can't have one without the other.

Bob: Can you tell what tune they're playing?

Mike: You don't even hear that.

Bob: I'm heartbroken!

Mike: The more experienced you get at square dancing, the more attention you pay to the band, and not quite as much to the caller.

Bob: So most people who square dance don't really hear what the band is playing. They know they're playing; they keep the beat, and it's a nice tune, but that's all?

Mike: I guess it's insulting to tell you what the band does. They could be the best band in the world, but without a good caller, the band's nothing. Now a good caller with a bad band could possibly make a success. It's doubtful, but more possible than the reverse.

Bob: Yeah, we did a square dance one time. Hughie was sick; Joe was drunk; I got drunk, and there was Matthew, sober. I tried to keep the beat on the guitar while propped up against the wall. It was a wonderful show.

Mike: And a good time was had by all!

Bob: But the people enjoyed themselves; they just loved that fiddle.

Mike: That's all you really need for a square dance—a caller and a "fiddlist."

The Keys Used in Oldtime Playing and Basic Fingering

Square dance fiddling has shaped the styles and techniques of players in many ways. Since there is little need for a fiddler to develop beyond the demands of his music, dance fiddling has, in a way, confined players' techniques to those it requires. An example of such a limitation is the paucity of keys in which the oldtime players like Harry are fluent. Since there is no vocalist who requires the adaptation of tunes to his vocal range, nothing compels the fiddler to render tunes in keys other than those which offer relatively easy fingering. With the open strings being G, D, A, and E from the bottom (see diagram 5.1), keys which give the fiddler the opportunity to frequently employ these tones as prime or essential intervals in the melody require minimal left-hand proficiency. Additionally, since it is desirable to drone open strings, keys which can utilize the tones of open strings for drones dominate the fiddler's repertoire. Invariably, therefore, traditional dance tunes are played in the keys of G, D, A, and C. The most frequent are G and D; A and C are somewhat less frequent. Occasionally a tune may be rendered in F or B flat, but these occurrences are rare. The keys of E flat, A flat, etc., are virtually nonexistent among traditional tunes played in a traditional way.

Since there is an overall similarity in fingering these few keys, they require only minimal fingering hand development. A fiddler who is unable to read music learns to finger tunes not so much from a clearly defined knowledge of the notes he must play, but instead by locating the position or place on a string where he must finger in order to obtain the tone he desires. To make sure his finger will be able to find its target each time he attempts to play a specific tone, the fiddler places his hand in such a position that whenever he depresses his finger there is a predictable, consistent result. For example, when he uses his first finger, he is usually striving to effect the tone one whole interval above the open string. The accompanying diagrams show which strings are fingered at what positions by each finger in order to play the notes in the first position. There are seven positions which the classical player moves to as he plays notes at different places on the fingerboard. The first position is the one where the hand is closest to the nut. Positions other than the first are almost totally foreign to square dance fiddlers.

The line marked *nut* in the diagrams is the open string; 1*L* and *H* are fingered by the first finger; 2*L* and *H* are fingered by the second finger; 3*L* and *H* are fingered by the third finger; and 4*L* and *H* are fingered by the fourth finger. Diagram 5.2 shows the notes in the G major scale, diagram 5.3 the notes in the D major scale, diagram 5.4 the notes the C major scale, and diagram 5.5 shows the notes in the A major scale. Notice that in all cases the note effected by the fourth finger can be played on the next higher open string. It is not surprising to find that most oldtime fiddlers rarely use their fourth finger, preferring to play the next higher open string instead. This assures accuracy of the tone and permits a shortcut in technique—that of developing the accurate use of the fourth finger.

Notice that in each key, G, D, A, and C, the first finger with only one exception

5.1 Fingerboard Diagram

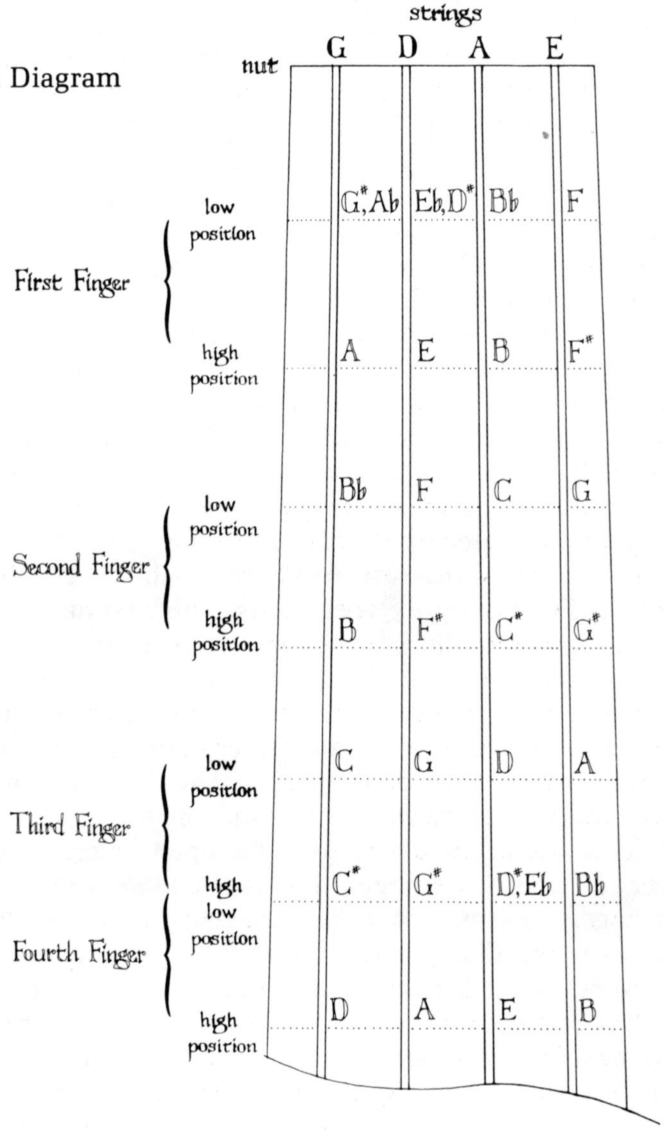

5.2 G Major Scale

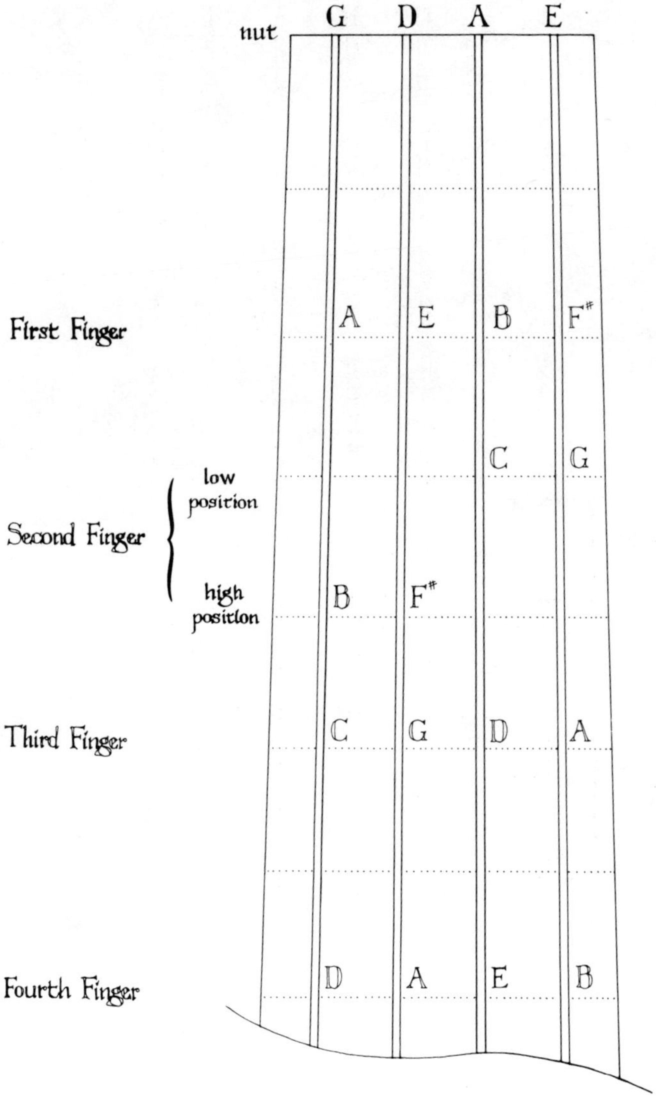

5.3 D Major Scale

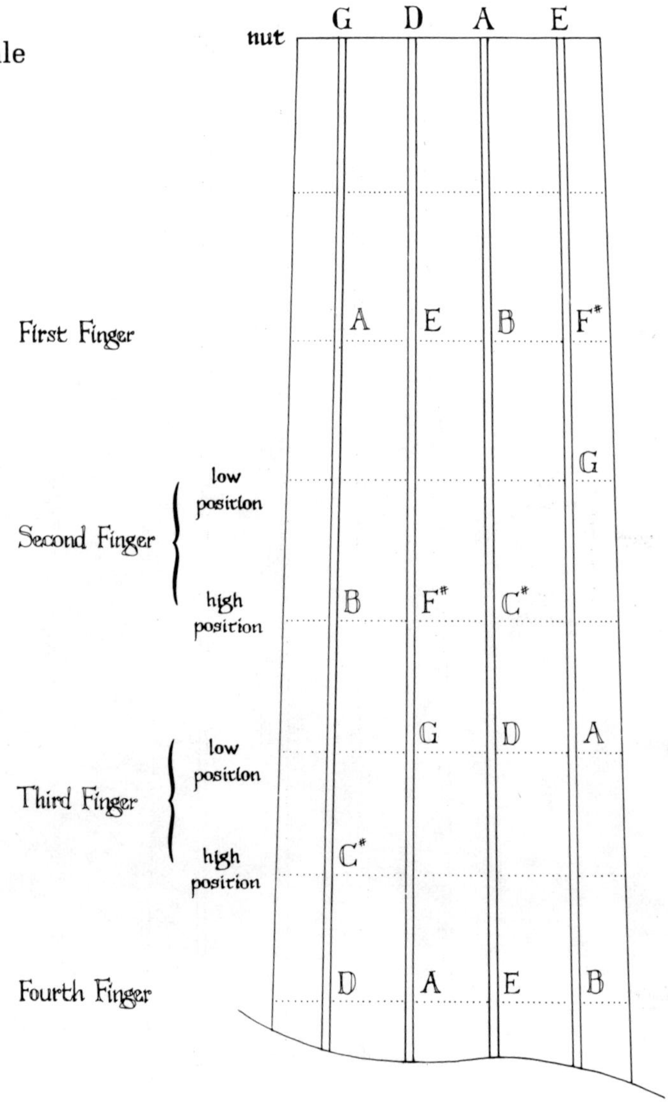

5.4 C Major Scale

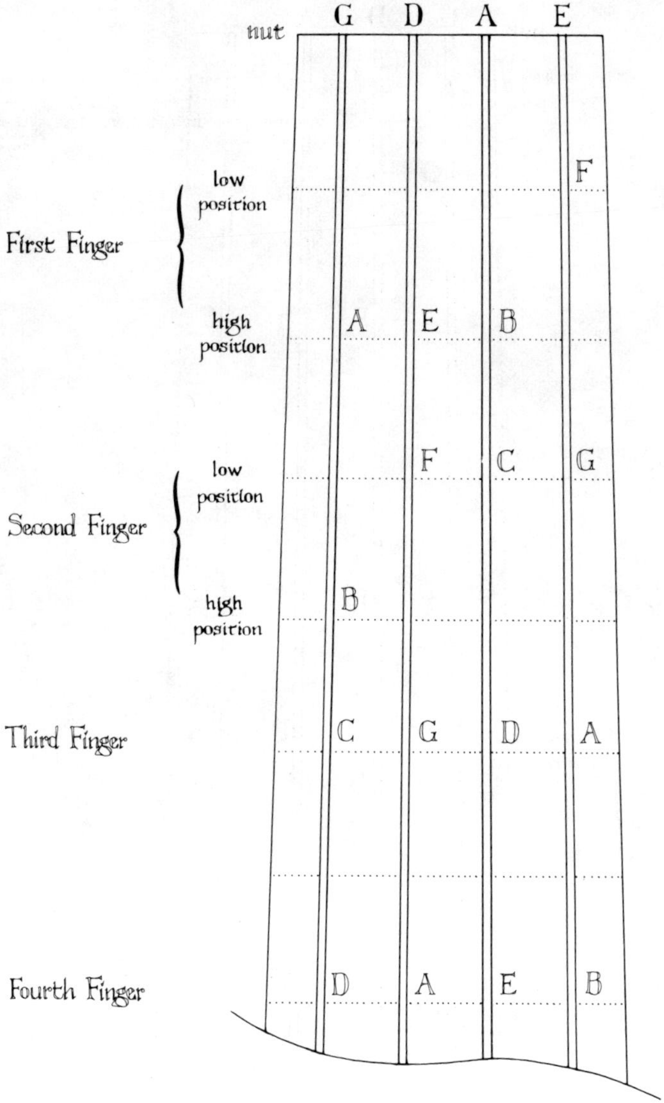

5.5 A Major Scale

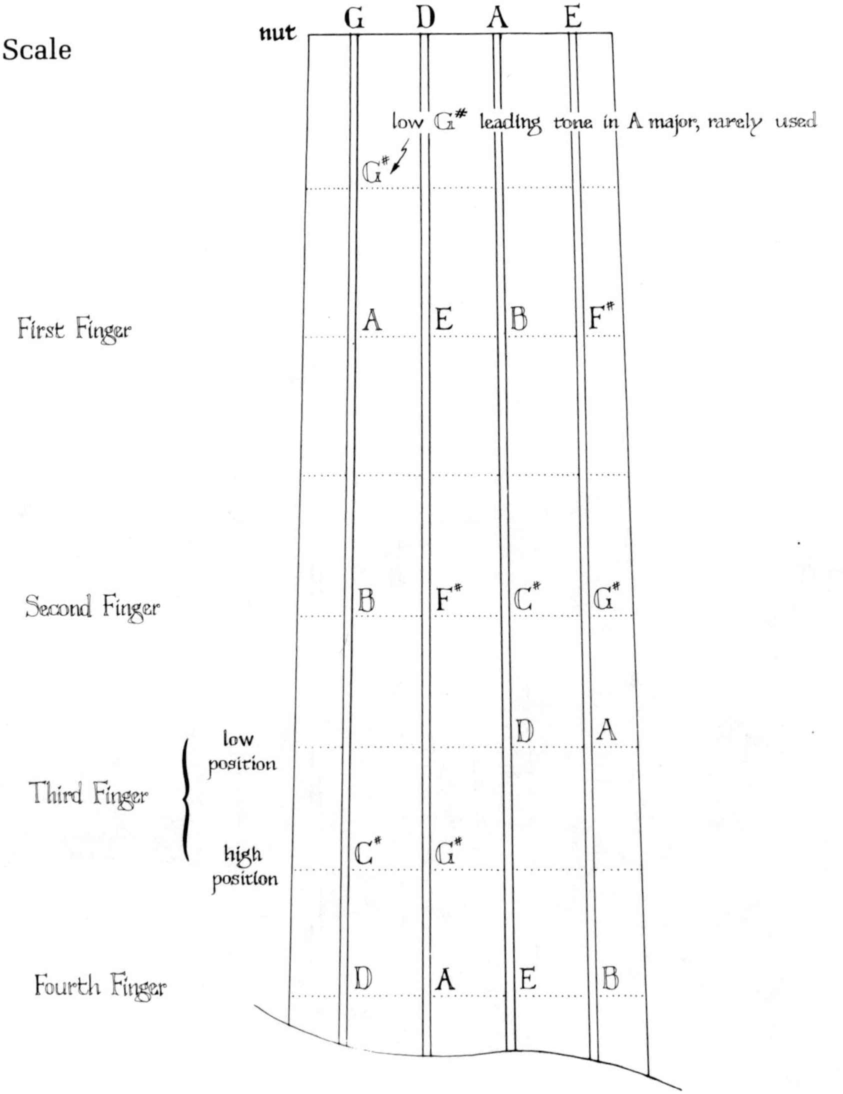

stops at the *1H* position. The exception is the note F on the E string in the C scale. It requires that the first finger stop at the *1L* position. This exception is not as important as one might suspect, since that particular F is often avoided in tunes in the key of C. Furthermore, when it is played, this fourth interval in the key of C is likely to be either a high F or even an F sharp used merely as a passing tone. Consequently, the first finger still does not have to deviate from the *1H* position.*

Examining the domain of the third finger, notice that it has charge of playing notes at either the *3L* or *3H* positions. In the keys of G and C, the notes in the scale which must be stopped by the third finger are always at the *3L* positions. In the key of D, only the C sharp on the G string requires using the third finger at the *3H* position. Once again, however, this particular C sharp is only rarely employed by tunes in D. I cannot think of even one case throughout Harry's repertoire, "The Kingdom" being one example, where that particular C sharp is used. In actual practice, then, in the key of D, the *3H* position need not demand the attention of the third finger since C sharp on the G string is simply avoided.

The key of A requires that both a C sharp and a G sharp on the G and D strings, respectively, be fingered by the third finger at the *3H* position. Once again, in tunes in A fiddlers seldom use these two particular tones; C sharp especially is avoided, except when it is used in a shuffled double stop like  .

Actually, A tunes in the oldtime repertoire sometimes avoid the G string entirely.†

Tunes in the keys of F and B flat can hardly avoid tones that require noting by the first finger at the *1L* position. Sharp keys of more than three sharps generally cannot avoid those tones which must be noted by the third finger at the *3H* position. Reviewing, we see that tunes in the keys of G, D, A, and C can be played usually without the first and third fingers having to deviate from the positions *1H* and *3L*, respectively. This consistency allows the positioning of the hand in such a way that whenever the first and third fingers are depressed, they will always land

*I found only a few tunes in the key of C so I cannot offer examples I collected. I believe, however, a glance at any American tune collection will bear out this generalization. See R. P. Christeson, *The Old-Time Fiddlers Repertory* (Columbia: University of Missouri Press, 1973), especially entries 58, 60, 61, 64, 65, and 66.

†There were not many tunes which Harry played in the key of A. One was "Devil's Dream," in which the G string is entirely avoided. His "Devil's Dream" also avoided the G sharp on the D string. For more examples see Christeson, entries 9, 10, 11, 12, 13, and 15.

at the same place (1*H* and 3*L*). Through rote a player establishes these as stable points of reference.

The problem of having to use the second finger equally often at the 2*L* and 2*H* positions, even in the easily fingered keys, forces the fiddler to pay particular attention whenever he uses his second finger. Within any scale, the second finger often has to note at both positions. I noticed that Harry is less than conscientious about the accuracy of his second finger. Since he shows no special concern about finding position 2*L* or 2*H* exactly, the result is often a note of inaccurate pitch. Some of a fiddler's apparent misnotings may actually be intentional neutral tones. Inasmuch as the fiddle has no frets, the fiddler may slightly flat or sharp certain scale intervals. These tones, however, are not confined to second-finger notings.

The diagrams point to another similarity among and within the keys of G, D, C, and A. Many fingering patterns have parallel adaptability. In a particular scale not only are the relative fingering positions often identical between neighboring strings, but in many ways the fingering patterns between keys are parallel. Notice that the fingering pattern on the G string in the key of G is identical to the pattern used in the key of D on the D string. Likewise, the pattern on the D string in the key of G is not only identical to that on the G string, but also identical to the pattern on the A string in the key of D. There is as well an identity between fingering patterns in the key of G on the A and E strings and the pattern in the key of D on the E string.

With this overlap or recurrence of fingering patterns within and among keys, a melodic sequence played in the key of G on the G string can easily be transposed to the key of D by merely using the D string. In either key, all the notes in the sequence will bear an identical relationship to the tonic. This parallel adaptability of fingering patterns offers little incentive to explore keys other than those in which the most frequently used sequences can be most often employed. It is possible to play a tune in G, and then to spontaneously transpose that entire tune to the key of D. All the player needs to do is begin on the next higher string and retain the identical relative fingering patterns. Transposing to A from G is not as easy and requires a more complete rearrangement of patterns in order to retain the original melodic sequence, unless the tune, in the key of G, can be played on just the G and D strings. In that case, the tune can be transposed to A by simply playing it on the A and E strings.

The similarity in melodic sequences among tunes can permit a player to be fluent in the keys of G and D especially, and A and C somewhat, without having to learn entirely new fingering patterns for each sequence in each key. Remembering that the fingers, with the exception of the second finger, fall consistently at the same positions in the keys of G, D, A, and C, one can see why and how oldtime players have great fluency in some keys yet lack fluency in others. Coupled with the fact that droning is most effective in certain keys (G, D, A, and C) and that there is little beyond individual desire to encourage the mastering of other keys, it is entirely understandable that dance fiddlers like Harry are tied to a few specific keys and the ornaments and patterns inherent in them. Since the role of the dance fiddler is to provide an audible rhythmic backdrop for dancing, there is little need for players to develop or refine more technically demanding potentials of their instrument.

Coordinating the Tune and the Call

The art of playing for a dance can be much more complex than merely mastering musical styles and techniques. The fiddler should play an active role in coordinating the music to the caller's instructions and, with nearly fifty years of experience, Harry has developed the art of playing dance music to a fine degree. Most fiddle tunes are composed of two distinct parts. Each part has specific calling instructions designed especially for it. The fiddler must pay attention to the dance and seek to keep his progress with the tune the same as the dancers' progress. As a fiddler, my attentiveness to such detail has been far too lax. I usually just play along with the band, leaving any coordinating to the caller. Harry explained that the fiddler's job should be more.

Harry: [Plays the "Irish Washerwoman."] You had to go over that four times till each couple's out, see, then they'd all make their lady-round-lady and gent-round-gent. Then you go [low part of the tune]. Now you do that four times, then you go [high part of the tune]. Then they're all back in their places again. "Oh Lady out to the right of the ring" [low part of the tune].

Bob: Can you call the dance too?

Harry? No, I never could call, but Mr. [forgot last name], he was wonderful. He said that I was the only fellow who ever played it right cause I didn't get into the high part before it was time. See, you let every first couple out, third couple out, fourth couple out, see, then they promenade, then they come back, and like the same way as the first two ladies cross over. Boy, that's a beautiful dance, but the music goes with the dance, see. [Harry fiddles, "Good Bye, Old Rover, Good Bye," high part.] Now you do that four times. That's the first two ladies cross over, then you go [high part] then start over.

Matthew: What was that tune?

Bob: "Good-Bye All Over"?

Harry: "Old Rover:"

Matthew: What was the dance they did to that?

Harry: "First Two Ladies Cross Over," the same with "Pop Goes the Weasel." You know you play that four times and then the chorus.

Matthew: You play that four times?

Harry: Yeah, then you go [high part] and then promenade there [high part], and if they ain't quite around, you do it again.

Matthew: I have a lot to learn about playing for a square dance.

Bob: Oh, really?

Matthew: I never paid attention. . . .

Harry: Oh, yeah, you got to pay attention. . . . I wanted to be right aside the caller when we used to play, you know. The music goes with the call, see?

When the dancers know how to dance, teamwork between the caller and the fiddler is greatly facilitated. Few sets fall behind in executing the dictated maneuvers if they are familiar with the calls. This allows the tune to progress on schedule, everyone being ready for the impending call as that part of the dance comes around. From my experience, the popularity of square dancing seems to have waned. Nowadays it is not uncommon for the caller to have to teach or at least review the calls before he can proceed. Consequently, the dancers are often unable to immediately and accurately follow the caller's directions. Harry has noticed that even when folks do know the calls they do not seem to have the enthusiasm that square dancers once had.

Harry: An old fashioned square dance was really something, but today they don't have the step anymore, they don't.

Matthew: They don't know how to do it.

Harry: I'd just like to show you the real step if I can. Just let me have some music over there. [Harry went over to his cassette recorder and put on a tape of some friends playing "Bummer's Reel."] I'd like to show you how they used to dance. They don't have no step anymore or nothing, you know. It was like this, see. Today they don't do that. That's old fashioned square dance step.

Goodbye Old Rover, Goodbye

var. for measure 2

Harry very deliberately showed us the proper "step." He placed one foot in front of the other with great care. Harry was clearly disappointed at the lack of effort with which people now dance.

Bummer's Reel

The Friday night square dance used to be more than just a square dance. Three square dances were usually followed by three round dances. The round dances included polkas, waltzes, and schottisches. For the square dances, traditional reels, jigs, and hornpipes, as well as occasional popular song airs, served as the musical accompaniment. Of the tunes Harry played for us, the square dance pieces were by far the most numerous. Here, using Harry's titles, is a list of all the tunes Harry played for us.

Bummer's Reel
The Kingdom
Old Nellie Grey
Soldier's Joy
Redwing
Fisher's Hornpipe

3 by 6 and Waltz Around
Sweet 16
Oh Mother It Hurts Me So
The Rochester Schottische
The German Schottische
Come Haste to the Wedding
Rag Time Annie
Flop-Eared Mule
Turkey in the Straw
Marching through Georgia
Finicula
Tarantella
The Mockingbird
Pop Goes the Weasel
Eighth of January
Beer Barrel Polka
Rickett's Hornpipe
Devil's Dream
Over the Waves
Blue Danube
The Campbells Are Coming
Irish Washerwoman
Maple Sugar
Arkansas Traveller
Mississippi Sawyer
The Russian Gallop
Buffalo Gals
The Girl I Left behind Me
Chicken Reel
Merry Maiden Polka
Pennsylvania Polka

Harry learned many of the pieces he used for round dances from his father, who played the accordion. Bob and I were frequently reminded that waltzes were among his father's favorite tunes. Harry was surprised at our interest in nonhoedown numbers, but he gladly played them for us. One of Harry's favorites was "Over the Waves."

Another dance Harry used to play is the schottische, which is now just about extinct in the Buffalo Valley. Harry said that even when he was growing up not many people could do the dance, but he always enjoyed playing for it.

Bob: Play a schottische.

Harry: Well, I like that "German Schottische." That's really a nice one. They danced to that, they danced a regular schottische dance, and not many people could do that. They'd one, two, three, and they'd . . . only a few people in it, you know. I played one time over here at the recreation place, over there at the penitentiary. There was an old German fella there, and I played. . . .

Bob: You told me about. . . .

Harry: Well, I played that waltz for him too, but then he wanted that there schottische. And boy, was he ever good, and gosh, he was about seventy-five years old. [Harry played the "German Schottische."] That really is something to see them; how they danced that, you know.

Over the Waves

German Schottische

Bob: Did they dance it side by side, or did they face one another?

Harry: Yeah, they'd be, well, like there'd be two couples to it. They'd be facing each other. See, they'd make these steps like two, three, four. I forget how they done it. Then they'd swing their partners, you know. Then they'd make a schottische dance. Nobody called it that though; there was no call'n for that whatsoever.

Bob: I see, almost like ballroom dancing?

Harry: Yeah.

Matthew: Did you ever play a clog?

Harry: Well, "Turkey in the Straw" could be called a clog.

Matthew: Were there people who danced a clog to it?

Harry: We had fellas that, well, they'd clog while everybody's square dancing. We had a couple guys who done that, yeah.

Matthew: Did you ever see anybody play the fiddle at the same time clogging with their feet?

Harry: Yeah, was somebody used to play over the radio. Some lady used to clog and play the fiddle at the same time.

Matthew: Can you do that?

Harry: No, I used to clog when I was young. I used to dance a clog. . . . Did we do the "Mockingbird" the other time you was here?

Matthew: I don't know it.

Harry: You don't know it? Oh, gee. That's really beautiful.

Matthew: I'd like to hear it.

Harry: Well, go on. Get your fiddle. We'll see if you can follow. We'll play it real slow [Harry fiddles a phrase] it's in D. [Harry plays "Listen to the Mockingbird."]

Matthew: That's a nice tune.

Harry: Well, that was the last tune we used to play when they finished dancing for the night. You know, then they called "Kiss Her in the Moonlight." Yeah, I used to know a lot of tunes. Gee, I really forgot a lot of them. There is an Italian tune, too. It's almost the same as "Irish Washerwoman," but it's called "Tarantella" [Harry fiddles the tune]. Isn't this a minor key? [Harry plays it again.]

Bob: That's a pretty piece.

Harry: Boy, oh man, you could really pick it off to that one.

Bob: What dance did you do to that?

Harry: Well, that is an Italian piece. I never played that one for a square dance, but sometimes you'd have groups of my relations from different places, and they'd want to dance the different dances.

Bob: They had a dance they did to that?

Harry: Oh, yeah, oh, yeah, it's a regular Italian dance. There's some beautiful Italian tunes like "Santa Lucia," "O Sole Mio," and "Finiculi." Did you ever hear anybody play them?

Matthew: What's that?
Harry: "Finiculi, Finicula" [Harry fiddles a phrase]. Ever hear of that?
Matthew: I've heard the tune.
Harry: Did you?
Matthew: Yeah. When you played it.
Harry: Did you ever hear anybody play that "Russian Gallop"?
Bob: No, I'd like to hear the "Russian Gallop."
Harry [Fiddles "The Russian Gallop"]: I missed a note there.

Harry's musical interests are diverse. However, since he is so accustomed to playing traditional square dance pieces, deviation from this medium severely taxes his technical abilities. Harry replaces long, sweeping bow strokes required by some nonhoedown tunes with his less-than-smooth square dance strokes. Regardless of the outcome, Bob and I were always encouraging and attentive listeners, and we insisted on taping even the least polished of his numbers.

Tape recorders did not frighten Harry. He himself frequently taped the sessions. The only time I sensed uneasiness in Harry was on the day we brought a fairly sophisticated tape recorder—a large reel-to-reel tape deck, two conspicuous microphones, and two large microphone stands—instead of our usual cassettes. Explaining that we hoped to get a good quality recording for the library, we cleared our intentions with Harry. Things went smoothly for about an hour. When we were through most of his repertoire, Harry began to get tired and somewhat suspicious of our motives. After all, we had never been so concerned with recording quality before. Sensing Harry's growing anxiety, we took a break and again explained that our motives were entirely honorable. We had no intention of using anything we recorded for commercial purposes. Furthermore, if these recordings ever did elicit commercial attention, any revenues would, of course, be funneled back to him, the performer. This seemed to quell Harry's worries, and we were able to conclude the session on the best of terms.

Bob and I developed excellent rapport with Harry and eventually with his wife, Evelyn. Harry was proud of his playing. Complimented by our interest in his fiddling, he took wholeheartedly to the role of teacher. Our greatest obstacle was in overcoming Evelyn Daddario's initial apprehension. Whenever we showed up, she reminded Harry of his promise to take her for a ride. For the first several visits we never even saw her. One day, however, Bob stopped by with a friend. Mrs. Daddario finally emerged and "struck up" a conversation with her. From that time on, Mrs. Daddario, affectionately known to us as "Mrs. D," always made an appearance.

One afternoon we stopped to see Harry unannounced. It was a beautiful spring day and we hoped to do some playing on the porch. I had just gotten an old Gibson mandolin and was eager to show it to him. Unfortunately, Harry was not in. He was out "loosening" the wheels of his '49 Ford. Assuring us that Harry would be back in a minute, Mrs. D led us on a half-hour tour of the flower garden beside the house while listing all the demands people had recently been making on Harry's time. Everybody seemed to want something from him. Some professor from over at Bucknell had been asking Harry to play square dances with him. She explained, "You know, just about everybody is after Harry's fiddling, being that he is so good." It was rewarding to have finally won Evelyn's confidence. She realized that far from being threatening, a serious study of Harry's playing was flattering.

Finally, Harry drove up in his gleaming black '49 Ford. The picture of Harry driving along in that old car is one that will stick with me forever. He pulled up in front of us, said hello, and then drove up, turned around in the driveway, and eventually parked in front of the house. Harry climbed out, offering his age-old greeting that he was about to take Evelyn for a spin. He also had to deliver some bows for rehairing to Mr. Levy in Williamsport. Harry was sorry that he could not spend more time with us, but perhaps we could get in a few tunes and a peek at my mandolin while Evelyn was preparing for her ride. Harry was in and out of the house in about thirty seconds, bringing with him the fiddle he had recently repaired so that we could inspect his handiwork. After his workmanship brought our usual praise, Bob broke out his guitar and I unveiled my mandolin. Harry's eyes lit up. He had always wanted a mandolin like mine and, on seeing it, he decided it was time for him to buy one. I gave him the name and address of the place where I had bought mine and explained that the prices for old Gibson's had become absolutely outrageous.

We soon tuned up and lit into "Ragtime Annie." Every few minutes we stopped to change tunes. After about an hour of playing, Harry stepped into the house to check on Evelyn's progress. She had been ready for quite some time but was enjoying the music so much she did not interrupt. Furthermore, she was about to call off the ride so that we could keep playing. Harry could not do that; he had promised. But Mrs. D decided she could not tear Harry away from his playing. Harry and Evelyn went on, both giving in, until we could hardly tell who had wanted to take a ride in the first place.

We asked Harry and Evelyn to come out on the porch for pictures before we had to leave, but Mrs. D would not hear of it. Even with Harry's prodding and a little sweet talk from Bob, we could not maneuver her into the camera's eye. Bob and I decided to get going so the Daddario's could attend to their pastime. We packed our instruments. Then Mrs. D came out and gave us some chocolates for our ride. "You know," she said, "Harry, tell them about the time. . . ." Harry and Mrs. D were off again reminiscing. This time we heard about when Harry was supposed to play a concert with a pianist. Since Harry could not read music, he had to play his part by ear. Back then, Harry could pick up tunes almost as fast as they could be played. He was known as one of the best fiddle players in the region. One time he was even asked by a famous singer to join his band, but Harry turned him down to stay in New Berlin. As the stories rambled on, their two faces grew brighter and brighter, but it was getting dark and we had a fifty-mile ride ahead of us, so we tore ourselves away, assuring the Daddario's that we would be back soon. We also took that occasion to invite them to visit us in State College if they ever made it up our way.

A few months passed till I next saw the Daddarios. They were in State College and stopped by Bob's house so we could play some music. Mrs. Daddario sat patiently through tune after tune. Finally, Harry announced he only had time for one more. After about a half dozen "one mores" Mrs. Daddario dragged Harry off so they would not miss the dinner they had to attend. We reminded Harry of our fiddle contest, which was coming up in July. He assured us that he would try to attend, but he could not commit himself. Harry never did make it and it is a shame, for he could have easily walked away a little richer, as had most of our fiddlers. David Bell, Marvin Kratzer, and Elmer Shaffer swept the top three prizes of our first fiddle competition.*

I have been meaning to get down to New Berlin to play with Harry. We both always enjoy the sessions. I love to show off some of the fancy "licks" I have picked up, and Harry likes to check on my progress. Harry has shown me a lot of tunes and when we get together to play them, there is an indescribable warmth which fills the air. Every once in a while I slip in a bluegrass lick that I think will really impress Harry, but it invariably goes unnoticed despite its difficulty. With Harry smiling, the tunes just ramble on.

*See David Bell in Chapter 7, Marvin Kratzer in Chapter 6, and Elmer Shaffer in Chapter 8.

6

The Bluegrass Fiddler: Adding New Licks to Oldtime Fiddling

Exactly when fiddling stops being oldtime and starts being bluegrass is very difficult to pinpoint. Both styles are tied integrally to the playing situations common to each, but there is more that differentiates the two. While there is no clearcut definition which can completely distinguish bluegrass from oldtime, a comparison between the way an oldtime fiddler like Harry Daddario plays and the way a bluegrass fiddler like Marvin Kratzer plays may help us see the differences between the two styles.

Bluegrass is not an ancient music form; its beginnings can be easily traced. Perhaps a brief account of its origins will help us understand what bluegrass is and how it differs from oldtime.

Traditional folk musicians have long recognized the compatibility of combining the fiddle, banjo, guitar, and more recently the bass and mandolin. String bands with these instruments flourished during the late nineteenth and early twentieth centuries, reaching a peak in the 1930s. Their popularity grew to such levels that commercial recording companies began making and selling records of the most renowned of these string bands. Thus bands like Gid Tanner and the Skillet Lickers and Charlie Poole and the North Carolina Ramblers began to find their way onto phonograph platters in many American homes.

Essentially, these string bands were little more than glorified square dance bands relying predominantly on tradition for both repertoire and instrumentation. A modern piece occasionally found its way onto a band's tune list, but it was usually subjected to an oldtime rendering and it was invariably played in the keys of G, D, A, or C. Stringed instruments have an affinity for these sharp keys, as we saw in Chapter 5.

Out of this period emerged an innovator, Bill Monroe. In the 1930s he formed a band called the Bluegrass Boys from which the term bluegrass was coined. Monroe's voice was very high, and naturally he demanded that songs be played in keys compatible with his range. Keys like B, B flat, and E, which he often used, had been unheard of among traditional string bands. Transposing pieces to such keys had a revolutionary impact on the musical direction of the string band. While the guitar and the banjo players merely used a capo, the fiddle, mandolin, and bass players had to learn new fingerings.

The use of the mandolin in folk music was itself somewhat innovative. Monroe used it both as a lead and rhythm instrument. In the rhythm section its primary function was to "chunk" the chords of the tune off-beat or in syncopation with the rhythm established by the bass and the guitar. This rhythmic interaction helps to create the tense and driving cadence so characteristic of bluegrass.

Initially, Monroe's band used a frailing-style banjo, the most viable style available at the time. One day, however, Monroe had the good fortune of discovering a young banjo player named Earl Scruggs, who had developed a dynamic three-finger picking style which proved to be the exact melodic and rhythmic addition Monroe's new sound needed. Monroe immediately incorporated it into his ensemble.

Bill Monroe's arrangements of songs employed alternate or occasional renderings of the melody by lead instruments as well as the vocalist. During its solo, or "break," a lead instrument usually played an ornamented, perhaps improvised, version of the melody. For solos, Monroe sought variety by encouraging the exploration of the blues scale (discussed later) in addition to the fundamental mode(s) on which a melody was based. Working in the blues scale, along with having to play in keys like B, forced traditional musicians to develop new techniques. The fiddler, perhaps most of all, had to expand his capabilities beyond that required in traditional playing.

The impact of bluegrass on folk music has become progressively more widespread. At first, bluegrass was a regional phenomenon. During the 1940s it prospered mainly in the Southeast, from Kentucky to Georgia. Only occasionally did it attract interest from northeastern metropolitan areas. When rock 'n' roll, along with its chief proponent, Elvis Presley, arrived in the 50s, bluegrass suffered a severe setback. Once thriving, Monroe and the other bands which had picked up on his sound began to scramble for survival.

In the early 60s there was a nationwide folk music revival. Along with general enthusiasm for folk music there developed an interest in early string band and eventually bluegrass music. Enthusiasm for bluegrass built slowly, until the film *Bonnie and Clyde,* which used Earl Scruggs' "Foggy Mountain Breakdown" for its theme, boosted its popularity substantially. Since then most people have been aware of the hard-driving banjo and fiddle sound of bluegrass.

An awareness and appreciation of bluegrass did not affect traditional folk musicians outside the South until relatively recently. Many of the older fiddlers in the Buffalo Valley, like Harry Daddario, are even now only vaguely familiar with the genre. Never during their developing years were they subject to enough bluegrass for it to have had a significant influence on their playing. On the other hand, many of the younger players in the valley, like Marvin Kratzer and David Bell, have developed an interest in bluegrass and consequently moved stylistically in its direction.

When they first began playing the fiddle, all our fiddlers, young as well as old, concentrated on learning traditional fiddle tunes. The dance style invariably associated with these pieces could not help but shape a player's style and technique. Eventually, in their playing careers, the younger fiddlers, through increasing exposure to bluegrass, came more and more under its influence. For Marvin Kratzer in particular, bluegrass became an exclusive musical interest, so Marvin offers perhaps the best example of bluegrass fiddling in the valley.

I first met Marvin in the spring of 1972. During my last year in college I had taken up the fiddle with an eye toward playing bluegrass. There was a band in town, The Nittany Mountaineers, which played every Wednesday night at a local bar. The Mountaineers featured Fred, the banjo player and lead singer; Gwen, who played bass and sang harmonies; and Carl, who played guitar and also sang harmonies. Joining these three was a fiddle player who drove all the way from Winfield RD 1, over fifty miles away. That fiddler was Marvin Kratzer.

To me Marvin was the band. His fiddling excited me to an extent only an ardent bluegrass devotee can understand. From listening to bluegrass records and study-

Marvin lives with his wife and children in a trailer not far from New Berlin. Somewhat animated in his poses, Marvin enjoyed our taking his picture.

ing Marvin's playing, I started to understand the fiddler's role and saw how and why he played what he did.

Eventually, I met some people who had a vague acquaintance with the Mountaineers. I was sitting with them at one of the band's performances, when, at intermission, to my delight, Marvin sat at our table. I built up the courage to reveal that I was learning to play the fiddle, and I timidly asked Marvin for some help. Crushing my hopes, he offered the excuse that he lived too far away and rejected my request.

I continued to practice on my own and tried not to miss any opportunity to see Marvin perform. I gradually developed enough confidence to play with some other musicians in town. One of the first I met was Bob Doyle, with whom I eventually joined to start the Buffalo Chipkickers. Our affiliation grew to include an academic as well as musical interest in fiddling. With his parents living in the Buffalo Valley, Bob took it upon himself to "scare up" some fiddlers from whom I could learn and with whom we could look into the area's fiddling tradition. Since he lived in the Buffalo Valley, Marvin became one of our first targets.

By the time I met Marvin under these new circumstances, I had learned to play well enough to clearly understand and study Marvin's playing. My own tastes had led me to a somewhat more contemporary approach to bluegrass fiddling, but Marvin was, nonetheless, an excellent subject for our investigation. From the beginning he was protective of his reputation for being the best fiddler in the area and it seemed to me he often worried that I was stealing his licks. This was my first exposure to such an attitude. Players like Harry Daddario and Bob Cheeseman had been helpful in every way. After only about four visits with Marvin, we abandoned our interviews because his attitude had grown progressively less helpful.

In his late thirties when we began our association, Marvin had been playing for almost twenty years. As a learner, he looked for guidance among younger fiddlers since he preferred their "sound" to that of the older players. A fiddler from New York, Curley Ramsey, used to drive all the way to the Buffalo Valley for hoedowns. His tunes and licks were different from those of the dance fiddlers Marvin was accustomed to hearing. According to Marvin, Curley used to play with the Stanley Brothers, a Virginia-based bluegrass band.* He became extremely influential on Marvin's playing. He not only served as a model on which Marvin could pattern his fiddling, but he also offered occasional instruction.

*The Stanley Brothers, Ralph and Carter, became one of the leading bluegrass groups in the country. Carter died and Ralph went into retirement for a few years but has subsequently returned to the stage as Ralph Stanley and the Clinch Mountain Boys.

Marvin also played frequently with a bluegrass fiddler named Blaine Shover from McVeytown, Pennsylvania. His ability is well attested to by his having placed, more than once, ahead of Marvin in local fiddle contests. Blaine and Marvin play similarly. Both use very short strokes, and both prefer to bow each note in their tune versions. Moreover, both occasionally incorporate a blues scale when ornamenting bluegrass songs. While I had the opportunity of hearing Blaine only once, Marvin's description of his playing and deference for his prowess left his abilities and techniques clear.

Marvin comes from a very musical family. His father, Doyle Sr., plays the concertina; Doyle Jr., his younger brother, plays the bass and sings tenor; and his older brother, Dick, though he specializes on the mandolin, is an accomplished guitarist and a capable fiddler as well. Marvin himself is primarily a fiddler, but he has also reached considerable competence on the mandolin, guitar, and Dobro. Marvin actually started playing the mandolin before turning to the fiddle. The lack of frets and use of a bow at first caused him such frustration that he was often tempted to smash that "damnable instrument," which he now so cherishes.

After reaching an intermediate level of ability on the fiddle, Marvin began to attend bluegrass festivals where he refined his playing by studying other players. Bluegrass get-togethers always have times and places where musicians gather informally to "jam." These situations are invaluable to a player who is trying to learn, for they offer him an opportunity to both observe and question other players.

Much of the repertoire of the oldtime players in the Buffalo Valley is fairly standard. By traveling outside the region, listening to the radio, and getting to know those players who traveled into the region for performances, Marvin expanded his repertoire to include many numbers, especially bluegrass pieces, not common to the valley. As he developed the techniques necessary to play these tunes, Marvin absorbed the stylistic influences inherent in them. Several of the tunes we collected from Marvin Kratzer, listed below, especially the ones with an asterisk, are not common in the valley but were imported by Marvin, who learned many at bluegrass festivals.

Goldrush*
Old Joe Clark
Lost Indian*
Stoney Creek*
Pop Goes the Weasel
Little Home in West Virginia*
Black Mountain Rag
Foggy Mountain Breakdown

Boil Them Cabbages Down
Old Nellie Grey
Soldier's Joy/Two Rattle
Bonaparte's Retreat
Rag Time Annie
Flop-Eared Mule
Turkey in the Straw
Marching through Georgia
Redwing
Irish Washerwoman
Devil's Dream
Mississippi Sawyer
Cheyenne*
The Girl I Left behind Me
Red River Valley
Irish Washerwoman ($^2/_4$ time)
Cripple Creek
Blue Moon of Kentucky*
Orange Blossom Special
Arkansas Traveller
Beaumont Rag
Rubber Dolly
Listen to the Mockingbird
Buffalo Gals
Cacklin' Hen*
Chicken Reel
Eighth of January
Tennessee Wagoner
Maple Sugar
Billy in the Lowground*
Cajun Fiddle*

Marvin used to play for square dances where he performed the traditional pieces familiar to most dance players. Notice, though, that we collected a considerable number of pieces solely from Marvin, many of which are bluegrass tunes. There are several pieces which cannot accurately even be called fiddle tunes. "Foggy Mountain Breakdown" is a banjo tune, and "Little Home in West Virginia" and "Blue Moon of Kentucky" are vocal pieces. These examples more accurately demonstrate Marvin's current musical interests than do the oldtime tunes. He now confines his playing almost exclusively to bluegrass. Claiming that he never really could master its sound, Marvin no longer cares for the oldtime style. He explained to Bob what he thought was the difference between oldtime and bluegrass.

Bob: Marvin, in your opinion, what do you think is the biggest difference between the oldtime player and the bluegrass fiddler?

Marvin: The oldtime fiddlers usually play on single strings and have a different action on the bow from what they now have in bluegrass.*

*This is not a very accurate observation. Playing on two strings is common among oldtime players, but for them the range of double stops does not often extend much beyond drones.

Bob: Do you mean that bluegrass players will take an oldtime tune then speed it up? Jazz it up?
Marvin: Yeah.

While Marvin draws an overly simplistic distinction, he makes two important points: there is a difference in bowing and a difference in ornamentation between oldtime and bluegrass. Bowing in this instance is important as it relates to rhythm. Let us first examine the way Marvin bows.

Holding the bow with his thumb under the frog, Marvin presses very lightly. He uses the upper third of the bow almost exclusively and takes very short strokes, one for each note. His bow hair is fairly loose. Rhythmically, Marvin's bowing is quite different from that of oldtime players like Harry. While both bow practically every note, Marvin does not seek or rely on the rhythmic consistency or monotony associated with square dance playing. Harry's equal emphasis on each note leaves little room for rhythmic subtlety. Marvin, on the other hand, shapes each note by regulating its "attack" or intensity, and thereby adds color and variety to his passages. Marvin's playing seldom gives the impression of the mechanical repetition so characteristic of oldtime fiddling.

Marvin's rhythms are varied. For one thing, he may play a solo, perhaps improvised, using sixteenth notes almost exclusively, or he may hold some notes for a quarter-note duration. Like other bluegrass players, he has a variety of rhythmic ornaments with which he can embellish a piece. He may shuffle through a number of measures whose chordal accompaniment lends itself to double, triple, or even quadruple stopping. The shuffle may itself vary from being strongly syncopated to only slightly syncopated to not syncopated. One rarely finds such a range of bowing techniques and rhythmic ornaments among oldtime players like Harry Daddario.

Defining or describing bluegrass is a difficult if not impossible task. One learns to distinguish oldtime from bluegrass by extensively listening to and watching both kinds of players. Even then, the listener usually develops only an intuitive understanding. Each style imparts a flavor which reaches beyond a mere description of its bowing or ornamenting techniques. There are many different bowing styles within just the bluegrass genre, most of which spring from the traditional styles of different geographical regions. Taking fundamental techniques from the styles native to their areas, bluegrass players from widely differing backgrounds employ a variety of approaches when playing bluegrass melodies and rhythms. Thus we have long-bow stroke players and short-bow players, "bluesy" and intricately orna-

Foggy Mountain Breakdown

first time

menting major-scale players, all within or under the bluegrass umbrella. Tying bluegrass players together, however, are certain uniform characteristics of bluegrass fiddling. The rhythmic variety and subtlety of often very intricate bow work is one of these qualities. The approach to and situations in which ornamentation and imrovisation are applied is another.

Bluegrass players usually draw their ornaments from a larger stock, and they use them in a wider variety of melodic situations than do oldtime players. While oldtime fiddlers have licks which they use to embellish fiddle tunes, bluegrass players have them as well as others appropriate for ornamenting nonfiddle pieces. They also improvise much more freely and extensively. Such abilities spring from the broader demands placed on bluegrass fiddlers.

"Foggy Mountain Breakdown" composed by Earl Scruggs is perhaps the most famous banjo tune in the world. Recordings of this tune always include solos by lead instruments other than the banjo. During its break, the fiddle offers its own interpretation of the melody. It is neither feasible nor aesthetically desirable for the fiddle to reproduce, note for note, the banjo version. Through ornamentation, the fiddle essentially creates a new melody which is congruous with both the chords

and the melody of the banjo's rendition. Though it is possible for most fiddlers to improvise their solos, many pattern them after the fiddle break as played on the Flatt and Scruggs recordings.

Chordally, the piece is simple. It is based on the tonic, usually G, and its relative minor, E minor. At the end of the tune the melody moves to the dominant or D chord before finally coming to rest at the tonic. For the fiddler, such a structure offers few improvisational hindrances. Since the banjo player is expected to maintain the melody, the fiddler is free to be creative and imaginative. Let us turn now to Marvin's "Foggy Mountain Breakdown." When it was recorded, no banjo was present, only a backup guitar. Marvin offered a characteristically fiddle version of the tune. The first time through is a fairly simple statement of the melody which, the second time, is more ornamented.

Little Home in West Virginia—basic melody

Frequently using double stops, Marvin hugs the chords of the tune. Many bluegrass players ornament extensively and sometimes exclusively with double stops which, as in this instance, function somewhat like chords. Marvin further embellishes the melody with glissando and occasional runs of sixteenth notes.

Vocal pieces offer all the lead instruments an opportunity to embellish and perhaps improvise on the melody or chords. The instruments take turns playing their particular versions of the melody. The banjo is fundamentally a chord instrument and consequently bases its break most often on the tune's chords.* The fiddle, being melody oriented, has the option of basing its solo on either the melody or the chords. While Marvin did not stray much beyond the chords in "Foggy Mountain Breakdown," he followed the melody in "Little Home in West Virginia."

The uses of glissando and chromatic intervals are especially noteworthy in Marvin's "Little Home in West Virginia." Glissando is a technique which is only occasionally employed by oldtime players but often heard in the playing of bluegrass fiddlers. Another feature of Marvin's "Little Home in West Virginia" which is extremely rare among oldtime fiddlers and not even especially common among bluegrass players is the use of chromatic intervals in ornamenting. Marvin has not really developed a chromatic approach to ornamentation. Instead he once in a while, as in this instance, moves through flatted intervals in order to embellish certain of his pieces. In "Little Home in West Virginia" it seems no mere coincidence that those chromatic intervals which can be viewed as ornamental are the

*A melody-oriented banjo style known as chromatic has become quite popular. The ornaments employed are similar to those the fiddler uses. It is not uncommon to hear chromatic-style players render fiddle tunes exactly as the fiddler.

Little Home in West Virginia—Marvin's fiddle version

flatted third and major third, and the flatted and major sevenths. While Marvin does use an F natural or flatted sixth in the sixth measure, it is not ornamental in nature. Looking at the simple tune line, one sees that F is intrinsic to the melody.

Marvin's use of flatted thirds and sevenths could stem from his tendency to utilize a blues scale in ornamenting. The Dorian scale can serve as such a blues scale. The flatted third and seventh would cause no difficulties for Marvin, even though he is dealing with what is essentially an Ionian or major scale melody. Familiar with Dorian scale ornamentation, Marvin's fingers have no problem finding both the minor and major third and seventh intervals.

It is noteworthy that an Aeolian scale can also be used as a blues scale. One might not be surprised therefore to find the sixth flatted in certain ornamenting situations. For the most part, however, Marvin's blues scale ornamentation incorporates only the flatted third and seventh intervals.

Another interesting aspect of "Little Home in West Virginia" is the frequency with which Marvin uses double stops. Double stopping is not the exclusive domain of bluegrass fiddlers. Oldtime players utilize drones and double stops, but they do not have the variety at their command that most bluegrass players do. The double stops bluegrass players employ are used in many circumstances. They need not even include the tonic as long as they fit into at least an extension of the chord.

A bluegrass fiddler's approach to fiddle tunes also bears the identifiable stamp of the genre he represents. Traditional pieces are impregnated with his peculiar rhythmic and melodic ornamentation. Contemporary or authored pieces often involve somewhat advanced techniques. Fluency in nontraditional keys and playing in positions other than the first are both within the grasp of a skilled bluegrass player. "Cheyenne" is one of Marvin's favorite pieces. Its playing demands technical proficiency and musical knowledge beyond that of most oldtime players.

Cheyenne

var. for A

The first half of "Cheyenne" moves between the keys of G minor and G major. It is built on a series of scales and repeating ornaments. The chief difficulty in playing "Cheyenne" is that it requires a familiarity with G minor and B flat major fingering. The melodies are not complex. The second half of the tune is primarily in B flat major. Its first line is composed mostly of double stops. Its second line, the final line of the tune, is merely an assemblage of formulaic embellishments. In the last measure, movement from B flat to A in the pickup notes links the two halves of the tune: to repeat the tune a player need only descend one whole interval to G, which is the initial tone of the G minor half of the tune. While "Cheyenne" is in some ways a complex piece, which I believe is beyond the ability or understanding of most oldtime fiddlers, it is easily within the grasp of most bluegrass players.

Since fiddling is usually confined to the keys of A, D, G, and C, it is surprising to find a country fiddler so fluent in B flat and G minor. But bluegrass demands that a fiddler become familiar with practically all keys. Fundamental to bluegrass, one must remember, is its vocal orientation. Often built around a singer with a rather high voice, many bluegrass bands play in the nontraditional keys of B, B flat, and occasionally F and E. Since none of these keys is common in the oldtime fiddler's repertoire, square dance or traditionally reared players who wish to play bluegrass must familiarize themselves with them and their respective fingerings.

To a bluegrass fiddler, playing in B flat and its relative minor, G minor, is not especially difficult. Many players use a fairly simple technique in which they transcribe the knowledge of, or fluidity in, the traditional keys to the newer keys by a strategic placement of the left hand. Fretted instruments like the banjo and the guitar can play in any key using G, D, and C fingering, simply by employing a capo. The fiddler has no such option; however, he can use a technique akin to "barring" on the guitar or banjo.

To play in B flat, the fiddler fingers the A and E strings with his forefinger at the B flat and F positions, respectively. The finger is held in this position continuously (except in some instances when it may finger an E flat on the D string and immediately return to its previous position). The other three fingers freely note the necessary tones of the scale without this established point of reference being affected. The stable position of the left hand aids accurate and consistent intonation. Once a fiddler is thoroughly acquainted with this technique, he may easily transcribe many of the licks he uses in the key of A. A slight reorientation is all that is required to achieve fluidity on the E, A, and D strings. One difference is that the fourth finger

6.1 B Flat Scale

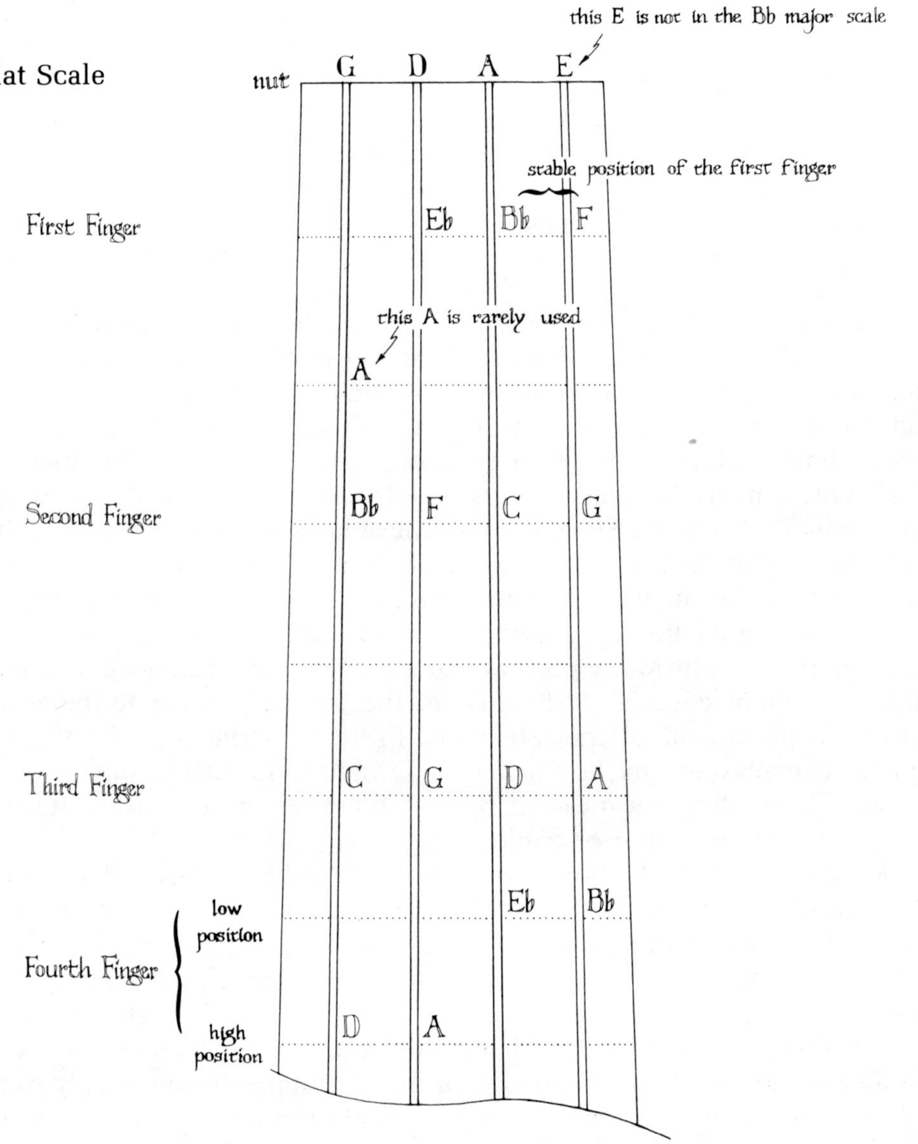

plays notes at its *L* position which in other keys is normally covered by the third finger. Notice too that the E flat on the G string is very high and would require of the fourth finger such a reach that the tone is either played by the first finger on the D string or avoided altogether.

To adapt this technique for playing in B requires only that the entire hand be nudged forward a half step. The fingers still note at the same relative positions.* The approach can be continued up the neck to include the key of C, offering a player two distinct positions, the first and the hybrid we have been discussing.

I cannot think of even one fiddle tune that any of our informants played in E (except parts of "Orange Blossom Special"), but I do know that Marvin had command of this key. Essentially, the technique which was used for playing in B and B flat is adapted for the keys of E and sometimes F. The first finger is placed in a stable position, stopping an E on the D string and a B on the A string. The remaining fingers then take reference from the first finger to accurately find the notes they seek. Diagram 6.2 shows how and where a fiddler places his hand and fingers in order to play in E.

To play in F, a fiddler need only push his hand forward one half step, retaining all the relative finger positions. Notice that were a player to move above F to G, his hand would be in the classical third position. While a fiddler may occasionally depart from the first position or a hybrid position, it is almost always for only brief ornamental flourishes. Marvin, however, frequently employs a third position double stop,  , in the key of G. He usually takes the first position double stop,  , and slides up to the third position. In executing this slide, the fingers move from the first and third intervals of the scale to the third and fifth. Both can function as G chords. This is easier than it at first appears. In playing these double stops, the distance between the first and third fingers in the first position is almost identical to the distance between them in the third position. All the fiddler has to do to move from one position to the next is slide his hand up or down the neck without particular worry over the different spacings between the notes in the new position. As quickly as he invades the domain of the third position, however, the fiddler invariably retreats to the familiarity of more tried territory.

*While fiddlers I have encountered usually employ this technique for playing in B and B flat, some players may also be able to play in both keys, particularly in B flat, without having to depend solely on such a technique.

6.2 E Scale

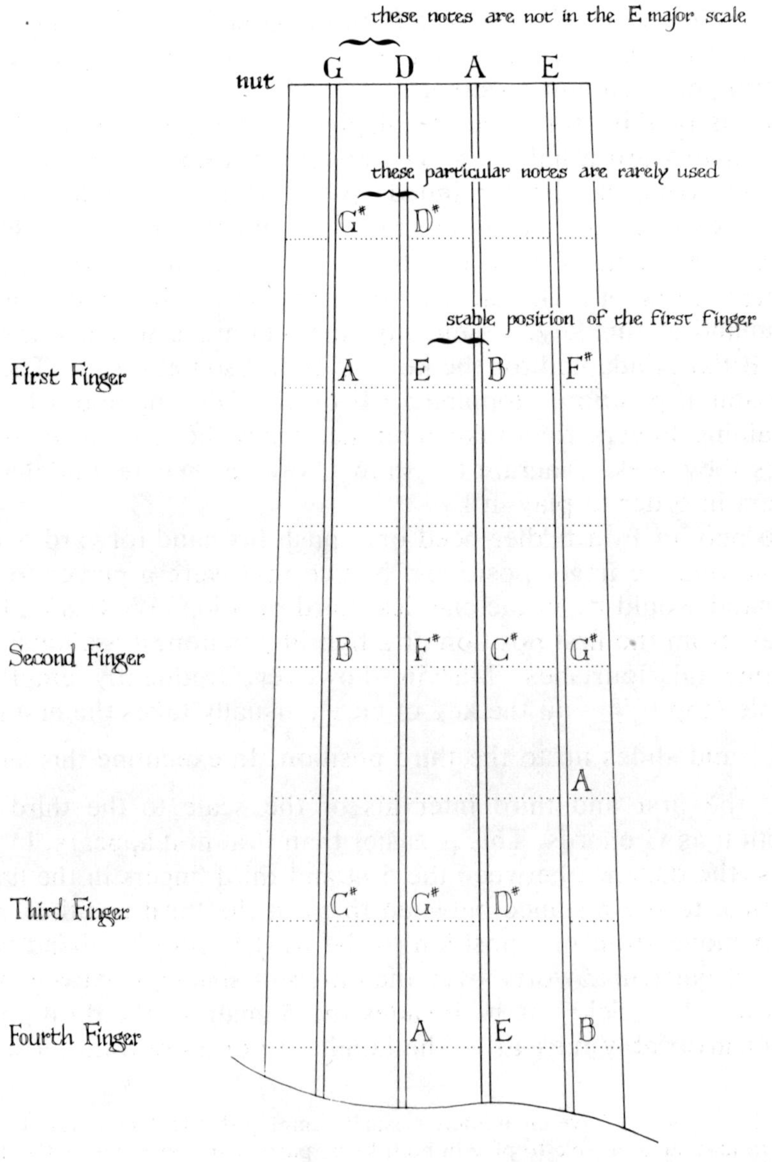
these notes are not in the E major scale
nut
G D A E
these particular notes are rarely used
G# D#
stable position of the first finger
First Finger A E B F#
Second Finger B F# C# G#
A
Third Finger C# G# D#
Fourth Finger A E B

6.3 Third Position for the Key of A

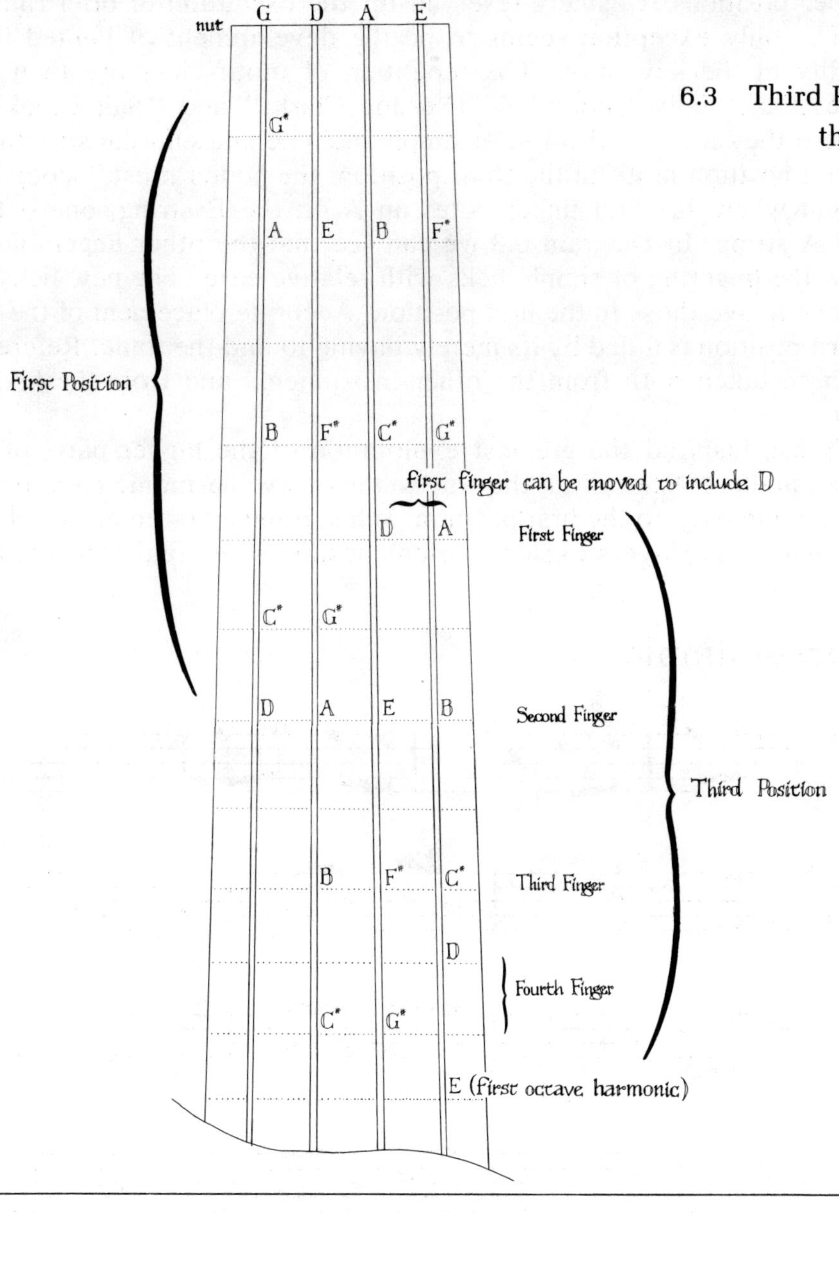

Travel to upper positions is usually reserved for the execution of brief runs or double stops. The only exception seems to be the development of limited third position capability in the key of A. The repetition of motifs in more than one position in tunes like "Sally Goodin'," "Old Joe Clark," and "Salt Creek" is facilitated because they are based on very simple melodic and chordal structures.

To repeat a first position motif in the third position, the fiddler must "scoot" his hand to the point where his first finger notes an A on the E string, one octave above the open A string. In Diagram 6.3 we can see that the other fingers are in position to allow the fingering of simple licks with relative ease. The new licks are usually one octave above those in the first position. Accurate placement of the first finger in the third position is aided by its merely having to find the tonic. Reference to the tonic can be taken both from the other instruments and from the fiddle's open A string.

The key of A has inspired the greatest exploration of the higher parts of the neck. I have seen fiddlers "shoot" all the way to the octave harmonic point on the E string and then jump back to the first position. While it must be remembered that some of the top bluegrass players explore various positions and registers for many

Old Joe Clark—simple

Old Joe Clark—ornamented

keys, they usually do not possess a clear understanding of them in a classical sense. High register explorations can be inspired by an effort to add just one "flashy" lick. The hand jumps to a note established by rote, carries out its mission, and returns to the safety of the first position (see "Old Joe Clark").*

Marvin observed that one difference between bluegrass and oldtime playing is the way the tunes are "jazzed up." To demonstrate, let us turn to a simple transcription of "Old Joe Clark," followed by Marvin's ornamented version. While the simple melody is clearly at the heart of this rendition, ornamentation is extensive. Four sixteenth-note sequences often replace two eighth notes or one quarter note. Retaining the gist of the melody, the "groups of four" clearly involve the simpler

*This technique is apparently not peculiar solely to bluegrass players. Sam Bayard explained to me that he had seen oldtime players do the same thing.

passages they replace. In the variation of measures 5 to 8 (last line of the transcription), Marvin demonstrates something we just discussed, brief flourishes into upper registers. Marvin jumps to the E, an octave above the open string, where he offers an interesting passage composed of sixteenth notes before returning to the first position. The second half of the tune is rendered almost exclusively with double stops. The rapid and frequent string changes result from a shuffle which both maintains the identity of the basic tune and provides a rhythmic and melodic contrast to the ornamentation used in the first half.

Bow ornamentation can easily enliven a tune. In "Listen to the Mockingbird" Marvin shows some of his more advanced skills. Intricate bow work is the outstanding ornamental feature in the second half of the tune. By shuffling, through B flat and B, he toys with a ragtime sound.

A series of sliding double stops provides a praiseworthy conclusion to each portion of the tune. Taking a G and a B double stop, Marvin moves to a B and D double stop on the same strings higher up the neck. Sliding back he plays a double stop, A and C sharp, which can be achieved only in this position. He finally comes to rest with a D and F sharp, which functions as a D chord.

Between the two major parts of the tune Marvin interjects an imitation of a mockingbird's song. By playing around very high on the E string, Marvin creates a believable imitation of a bird and turns this number into a showpiece.

Marvin is not incapable of fiddling in a style appropriate for square dancing. He has played for square dances on many occasions. Although his repertoire of traditional pieces is extensive, Marvin explained to us that he no longer enjoys playing the old tunes. Besides, he insisted, he could never really get the oldtime sound of the older players in the valley. There is something different about the bow work which always escaped him. Marvin seemed almost proud of this inability, for it supported his affinity for and insistence on playing bluegrass exclusively.

Bluegrass, like any other popular music form, is, and has been, subject to a variety of influences. It is not exactly the same as it was twenty years ago, nor is it likely to be exactly the same in twenty years as it is now. Already there are influences, like that of jazz, and especially swing, which are affecting the way many bluegrass musicians play, and let us not forget the inevitable influences that have not yet arisen. How thoroughly current influences will mold the bluegrass of the future remains to be seen. One can be sure, however, that the bluegrass fiddling of today will not be identical to the bluegrass fiddling of tomorrow, just as the bluegrass fiddling of today is not exactly the same as it was yesterday.

Listen to the Mockingbird

7

The Fiddler in a Musical Family

Folk music in general and fiddling in particular are harbored and perpetuated, in great part, within the family unit. The phenomenon of the "musical family" is no stranger to any of us. The proximity of members to one another plus their very early exposure to music has proven very fertile for maintaining fiddling and folk music. The Bells of Lewisburg are one such musical family.

Members of a musical family rarely specialize on the same instrument. Each usually chooses his instrument with regard to which instruments are already being played. In that way the family can join together into an ensemble. This instrumental diversity, evident among family bands like the Carters and Monroes, helps keep alive not only fiddling and folk music, but also the string band tradition.

Music in the Bell household is not the sole domain of the patriarch. It is a family experience enjoyed and participated in by all. Both David and his wife Laura were themselves born into music-making families and have carried on the tradition with their children. Laura grew up in the Bingaman family; her father and four brothers were all musicians. While Laura herself did not play an instrument, she invariably participated in the music-making as an encouraging listener. David, on the other hand, was an active bearer of his family's musical heritage. Learning from his father and uncle, both of whom were considered expert, David eventually became

The Bell Family: *left to right,* Laura, David, Dougie, Davey, and Dennis.

an accomplished fiddler. He has recently even expanded his musical conquests to include the guitar, mandolin, and banjo.

The love for music stretches through many generations in both the Bell and Bingaman ancestry. It was and still is a chief source of family recreation. Before the days of television people had other pastimes. Not privy to an upbringing which encouraged reading or other literary pursuits, many family members turned to music to while away their leisure hours. Playing music with one another strengthens the family bond and yields a cohesiveness many families nowadays seem to have lost. Talking about this, Clarence, Laura's brother, said that music "kind of binds [families] closer . . . my parents always made us practice, you know, or tried to make us practice, but my older brother Lamar, he would go and be the one to begin to practice, and I'd be the one who wanted to go out and play ball. I don't know how it is now but back then you didn't have television. You didn't have so many things to follow, you know. Your own amusement would be something like an instrument, and if somebody got it and the other didn't have anything to do, he'd like to do it too." About his father, Clarence said, "He wasn't a great musician or anything like that, but he had music in him." William Bingaman played bass.

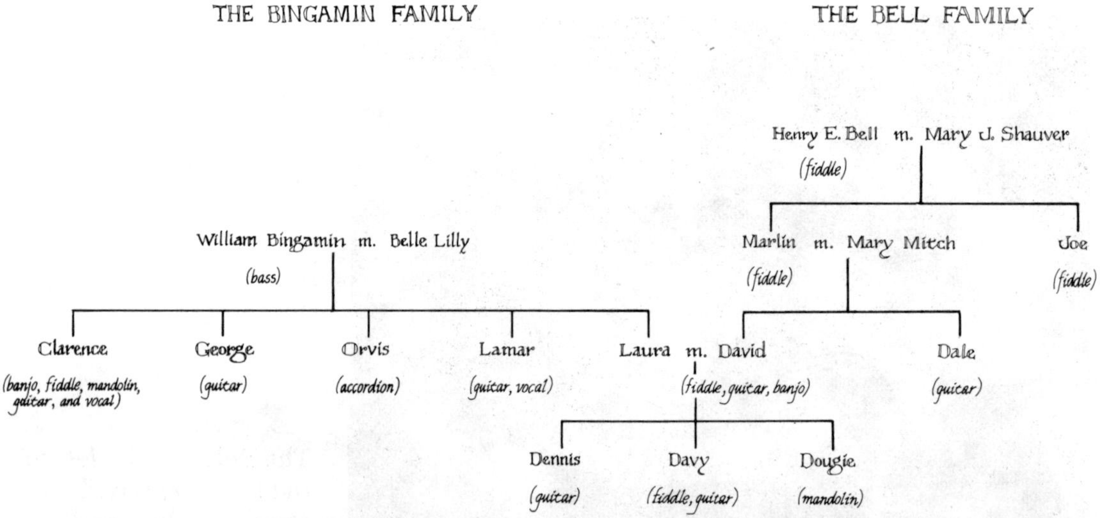

Traditional pieces form the core of the family musical experience for both the Bells and the Bingamans. Passed from one generation to the next, the old tunes have the highest survival rate. Regardless of which tunes are played, it is inevitable that the music enjoyed by one family is preserved by its succeeding generations. In the continuum from past to future, four generations of Bells have demonstrated how a folk music tradition is carried on within a family unit.

When David was a child he was irresistibly attracted to the fiddle, his father's instrument. Since playing the fiddle requires a maturity which his parents associated with the attainment of a specific age, David's father did not allow his son to try his hand at playing till long after David himself felt he was ready. To most parents, nonetheless, it is their intention for their children to carry on the art they themselves inherited.

Bob: It is interesting to me to watch how the kids take to these instruments.

Laura: This was our dream when the kids were born, when they were babies, when I was still in the hospital, we talked about playing.

Bob: You mean who was going to play what?

David: When this guy here [Dougie] was born, I said to her, "Hooray, I got a fiddle player!"

Bob: I guess as a father it would be kind of fun to play with the kids, wouldn't it?
David: Yeah, I think so.

The conversation then turned to how David first got started on the fiddle.

David: Well, in the first place, that's the only instrument my Dad ever had around the house.
Bob: Did he let you fiddle with his fiddle?
David: Nope. The way I learned to play the fiddle was when my Dad and Mom would go away, and often times us kids would stay at home. Mom and Dad would go to the store or something like that and I'd get the fiddle out. My Dad wouldn't let me have the fiddle when he was there.
Bob: Did he have only one fiddle?
David: Yup. He had only one fiddle and he wouldn't allow me to have it when he was there. But when they'd leave, I'd sneak it out and that's the way I learned to fiddle.
Laura: His kids daresn't touch his fiddle, but when Dave goes away they do get his fiddle out.
Bob: Yeah, and probably learn to play.
Dennis: How in the heck did you find that out?
Laura: Why, I live here, too.
David: It was a long time before I got a fiddle of my own. In fact, it hasn't been too awful many years ago that I got my own fiddle. I was using Laura's uncle's for a long time. I have it here yet. Then I finally went and bought my own over there at Moyer's.*
Bob: How old were you when you were sneaking the fiddle?
David: Well, I was six or seven years old when I sneaked the fiddle. Then when I got a little older, why when he'd [David's father] get the fiddle out, he'd set and play it, then hand it to me. Then I'd try it, you know.
Bob: Was he surprised that you could scratch out a tune?
David: Oh, yeah.
Bob: Thought you were really talented?
David: Yup, he thought I was.
Laura: You thought you were great, too, I bet.

*Guy Moyer, until very recently, sold and repaired violins and other stringed instruments. His shop was in Freeburg, Pennsylvania, about twenty miles from David's home.

David: I thought I was. I thought I was really good when I was ten years old. I thought I was something. And I had a job holding it, I'll tell you. But you know, when I really started playing the fiddle, I was probably fifteen, sixteen, along in there. I figured I learned to play it, and if anyone else wanted to play, they could learn to play, too, just like I did.

David has an enviable musical talent, but one must not underestimate the head-start he got by being part of a musical family. The very fact that he was interested in learning to fiddle at such an early age was a result of his being exposed to his father's playing. Let us examine how such a privileged child begins his musical endeavors.

Families are at the heart of the oral transmission process. From parent to child pass all life's values and goals, speech and expression, customs and attitudes. Recreational preferences are passed as well. Continually subject to musicmaking at home, a child will inevitably develop an interest in that which so occupies his parents. More than this normal process of socialization, specific family pressures insure a child's interest in music. Pastime preferences affect the child's relationship with other family members. In a family that depends on musicmaking as a fundamental source of recreation, the child must learn to participate. In Clarence Bingaman's words, "I heard everybody play music so I wanted to play, too, just like they did."

Playing an instrument is of course the means by which one can join the fun. Although some family members do not actively participate, as listeners they are involved in the family's musicmaking. While Laura neither plays an instrument nor sings, she maintains her presence among the group as an encouraging listener. She may have been kept from active involvement because she was a woman. In no generation in either the Bell or Bingaman family do the woman actively participate.* But for the boys in the Bingaman family, playing music was almost required. Laura's and Clarence's father played the bass and mandolin and he insisted that his sons play something. Laura recalled, "All I can remember is that my dad used to take them in a room and that would be it. They'd just sit there and play. When they were smaller he gave Lamar and Clarence lessons one time, but it was only until they'd got the chords and stuff. I guess that was the only lessons they've ever taken."

*I should point out that women do actively participate in many musical families.

Photo courtesy Penn State Information Service

David, Dennis, and Bob play in David's back yard. Dennis is playing the spoons.

Laura's brothers' proficiency, in spite of a lack of formal training, points to their having almost a predisposition toward music. Whereas they could, I suppose, possess a genetic advantage, I prefer to think that exposure to music from a very early age prepared them for their musical undertakings. By the time any of them actually picked up an instrument, he had already passed through several passive stages of development.

Through his early years, a child in a musical family like the Bingamans is continually exposed to music. As he listens to the playing of his parents and siblings, he becomes aware of its specific rhythmic and melodic qualities. He also begins to recognize the basic styles, repertoires, and roles of the various instruments. In this way the child cultivates a recognition and appreciation of the art before he tries to play.

Playing with a fiddle at a very early age provides merely an introduction to its physical and dimensional qualities. To a child, the instrument is, at first, just a toy. He does not understand that something very exacting must be done in order for music to be made on it. Only when he is big enough to hold the fiddle, that is, able to reach the strings with one hand and bow with the other, can a child actually experiment with trying to play it.

The time invariably arrives when the child grows old enough to be able to learn. Learning to play a musical instrument requires access to a model—one who plays the type or types of music the novice hopes to master. Musical families supply these models and at the same time offer constant guidance and encouragement. Children reared in musical families have distinct advantages over those who are not. They have an intuitive understanding of what to play from continual exposure to music. Years of listening have given them an immediate grasp of the fundamentals of the art and when the time comes for them to try to learn an instrument, assistance is readily available.

Happily for the family, children do not all choose the instrument of their father. Since they all intend to participate in group musicmaking, they usually diversify. Variety offers each participant the greatest opportunity for individual contribution within the group. The string band tradition which is so much a part of the family musical experience defines how the guitar, bass, banjo, mandolin, and fiddle interact. Each child decides how he would like to relate musically to the group and chooses accordingly. If someone has already picked the instrument he wants, the child is encouraged to pursue one that is not being played. Sometimes he insists on an instrument that another is already playing. The group in that case usually manages to adapt to the duplication of one of its ensemble.

Choices are usually restricted to the instruments and learning models available. Since their father is accomplished on the fiddle, guitar, banjo, and mandolin, the Bell children may choose any of these without having to look beyond their nuclear family for help. It is no surprise that each has picked his instrument with careful attention to those already being played.

Bob: Do you think when you get a little older that you'll be able to play music with your brothers?

Dennis: Yeah, if he learns to play the fiddle.

Bob: Now why does music flourish in your family, and how are the instruments chosen by your family members? You have Dennis. How old is Dennis?

Laura: Ten.

Bob: Davy?

Laura: He's twelve.

Bob: And Dave is teaching Davy to fiddle, right?

Laura: He's interested in the guitar, though.

Bob: Can he do anything on the fiddle yet?

Laura: Some.

David: He's done a little bit, a very little bit of "Twinkle, Twinkle Little Star."

Laura: Well, you start them out that way, you know, he was showing Den chords on the fiddle, too, you know, but Den was just bound for the guitar, and now Dougie, he just loves the mandolin. He had it out this morning, and he was strumming away for dear life. But Dennis is stuck on the guitar and spoons.

Bob: I think he is going to be your rhythm man. Do you think the music is taking with the kids?

David: I think so.

Laura: They love it.

Anticipating each other's concentration on different instruments, the Bell children have begun to diversify. Though he is working a little on the fiddle, Davy's primary interest is in the guitar. With Dad on the fiddle, there is no great need for a fiddler right now and besides, who could hope to compete with him anyhow? Right now, Dennis is leaning toward the guitar, too. This poses no problem since two guitars can easily be incorporated into the group. To round things out, Dougie has decided on the mandolin. Within the Bell family the continuation of the string band's traditional instrumental combination has been assured. The same was true in the Bingaman family. Clarence guessed that he and his brothers chose different instruments "because brothers, they learn one instrument and they didn't want to hear just one instrument by itself so they tried to get something else that would go with it."

A child or even an adult may begin an instrument that he later abandons for one he finds easier or more enjoyable to play. Davy initially followed in his father's footsteps by trying his hand at the fiddle, but he now leans more toward the guitar. Clarence Bingaman likewise started on the fiddle but later switched to the banjo.

Laura: Well, Clarence played the fiddle at first.
David: I guess that's what Clarence started out on, the fiddle. I guess it was because he used to play it on top of his head and behind his back.
Bob: Oh, he did trick fiddling?
Laura: He used to, oh yes. He used to do all sorts of tricks.
Bob: But he doesn't play anymore?
Laura: Not the fiddle. Clarence hasn't picked up the fiddle in a long time.
David: He laid down the fiddle and forgot about it.
Laura: When he started on the banjo then, that was it.
Bob: So the banjo is his principal instrument.
David and Laura: That's right.

Music affects friendships as well as family life. Children and adults exposed to music at home often seek the company of other musicians. Whenever the Bingamans threw a "shindig" it was bound to be a musical extravaganza and David was invariably a major participant. As a matter of fact, it was at one of these get-togethers that David and Laura met.

Laura: We used to get together over here at my Mom's on a Sunday afternoon, and used to hook up the speaker system outside, on my Mom's big enclosed porch. Well, it wasn't closed in then. Cars would park from one end of this road to another.
David: We'd be playing inside the house.
Bob: Is the house [pointing] down there?
Laura: Yeah, over here by the hill, the little farm house over here.
David: Lamar would hook up the speakers and stuff out on the porch. He'd have

one on each end of the porch. And we'd be playing in the living room. It would be going out so as you could hear it.

Laura: Cars would park, and set there and listen. This would go on, and my mother and I would get together and bake. Mom would bake bread and I would bake cakes. We'd make ice cream. Everyone had a ball, and I mean really a good time.

David: Yeah, we'd play a while, then eat a while, play a while, and eat a while.

Bob later asked how David had begun playing with the Bingamans.

Clarence: Well, David started playing with us before he started going with our sister. We often got together to play music. His brother and my brother were in the service together, and the one told the other of Dave playing the fiddle. You see, they didn't know each other until they were in the service.

David: They [the Bingamans] came after me and wanted me to play the fiddle for them.

Laura: And that's how I got hooked up with him.

Clarence: Me and Dave, and my brother and Dad, and we had a couple of other guys playing with us when we first started. Then when my dad died, I went to another band. Then my brother and me got back together again.

Even though she loved her family's music, Laura vowed never to marry a musician, especially a fiddler, because of all the time he spends with his instrument. Laura's intentions lasted only until her glance fell upon that remarkable fiddler who every Sunday joined her family.

Laura: And that's one thing, see, Mom stayed home a lot. She didn't go out when Daddy and the boys would go playing cause of us younger kids, my sister and me and the two younger brothers. I vowed I would never marry a guy who played music; I was not gonna sit at home for anybody, and now look what I turned out and done!

Bob: Who does an Admiral's daughter marry but some Ensign?

Laura: Yeah, I often said that to Mom. "Well, I'm not marryin' nobody that plays hillbilly music or anything like that, I don't want to be tied down and set at home like this." Well, Dave Bell come along, and that was that. [To Dave:] You came to my place in the wintertime and we didn't go together until July of that year, that was July of '52. I was really in love with him. I made cheese and macaroni (and) I forgot to put the cheese in. . . . I was baking a pie and asked Mom what kind to make. Mom says, "Well, make a plum pie." Okay, so I didn't take the seeds out. I baked a cake, and I never put the sugar in the damn cake.

Bob: You were in love!

Laura: Boy, where was my mind?

Bob: Now you remember to take the seeds out of the plums and put the sugar in the cake?

Laura: It's better all over.

David: Cheese in the cheese and macaroni.

Laura: He used to come up, and we'd never go anywhere, because he brought the fiddle and there they'd set.

David: And her brothers and I and her dad would—

Laura: All get together.

David: As soon as the meal was over, bang! Into the room we'd go and all get together and strum away.

Laura: Dave'd forget to go home and we'd find him sleepin' on the couch the next day.

Bob: What's it like to go out with a fiddler?

Laura: Oh, gosh, I don't know, I enjoy goin' out with him. It's no different now than it was when we were single and would go out. It really isn't. I feel real proud, though, I really do, that he plays like he does.

Playing instruments together forms a strong bond among family members and friends. Everyone enjoys homemade music. All are proud of both group and individual abilities. Till now we have only discussed the Bell family as musicmakers and tradition bearers. Now let us turn specifically to the kind of music the Bells play at home.

When we met, David Bell was in his mid-forties; he was born in the early 1930s. As he was growing up, David was exposed almost exclusively to the traditional or oldtime dance style of fiddling common to most players at that time. Stylistically, his father, grandfather, and uncle were all oldtime players. While David's father and grandfather confined their repertoires to traditional pieces, his Uncle Joe often experimented with the popular pieces of the day.

The oldtime tunes were the first ones David heard and learned; however, by the time he began to really "get into" the fiddle, he was fifteen or sixteen and bluegrass had started to make its way into the valley. Bluegass, still in its infancy, was broadcast from WWVA (Wheeling, West Virginia) and could be picked up at night in the Buffalo Valley. The newer pieces which David heard on the radio quickly attracted his interest. While he maintained the oldtime pieces in his repertoire, continuing to play them at home and at square dances, David increasingly directed his efforts toward learning bluegrass.

Many players with a background in oldtime fiddling have successfully adapted their styles to bluegrass. Bluegrass, being relatively recent in origin, at first had to recruit its fiddlers from the ranks of the oldtime players. As a new genre, bluegrass had to make do with what was available. Though his own playing was based more on an oldtime style, David managed to eventually cope with the newer ornamental and rhythmic demands of bluegrass. In Chapter 3 we used many of David's tunes as examples of ornamenting. ''Cripple Creek'' is particularly worthy of review because it demonstrates David's fiddling in a bluegrass setting.

David has yet to abandon the musical roots from which he grew. The oldtime square dance pieces in his repertoire have not been replaced by, but merely supplemented with, bluegrass numbers. Creeping onto his tune lists, novelty pieces like ''Bear Creek Hop'' show also that David's musical purview is confined to no narrowly defined genre.

Bear Creek Hop

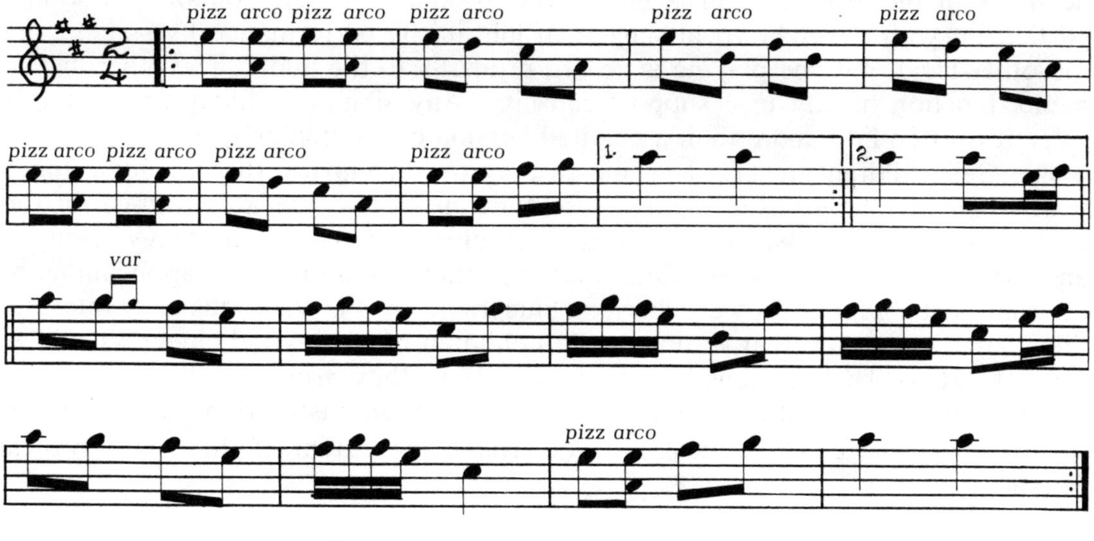

Fire on the Mountain

One of David's most dynamic pieces is "Fire on the Mountain." Known usually by bluegrass players, it is the piece with which David won the first fiddlers' competition held in conjunction with the Central Pennsylvania Festival of the Arts, on July 18, 1975, in State College.

It is not hard to understand why bluegass has such appeal among many traditional musicians. In group playing it offers all the members an active role. Not only do many of the instrumentalists have the opportunity to take solos, but also any participant with the right vocal range can join in the performance by singing. On the other hand, oldtime playing is geared primarily to the fiddle. The other instruments function mostly in a support capacity. Any singing is likely to be simple since it is often little more than a chanted version of the fiddler's tune.

The Bell children are first learning to play or accompany the old fiddle tunes which embody the stylistic elements so fundamental to the art. A grasp of the traditional pieces is essential for further development. However, Davy, Dougie, and Dennis will no doubt eventually attempt more contemporary applications of their musical abilities. They are learning bluegrass, for it is what musically interests their father most. Whether or not the Bell children reach beyond bluegrass will, to a great extent, be determined by their friends as they grow up. The family has provided them with both an interest in music and basic instruction on a variety of instruments. The children must now determine the extent of their own musical pursuits.

8

More Fiddlers and Their Ways: A Continuing Search

This book grew out of a research project that was conducted primarily between the fall of 1973 and the summer of 1975. Bob and I had the opportunity and financial assistance to record about ten players in and around the Buffalo Valley. We chose to concentrate on those players who were especially cooperative or whose playing exemplified specific characteristics we wanted to explore.

Marvin was the best example of a bluegrass player, Harry was one of the best oldtime players, Archie and Ralph were the most fruitful of the nonperformers, and David's household offered the clearest picture of the family's role in transmitting and maintaining folk music. We are planning to continue our search for new players and to preserve our friendships with those we have already worked with. In many ways our collection effort is an ongoing project which we hope will last for a long time.

Elmer Shaffer of Millheim, Pennsylvania, is one of the players we most recently interviewed. Bob and I had often heard that there was an excellent fiddler who lived in Millheim, but we put off visiting him until we had thoroughly covered with our other players the areas that most demanded our attention. It is hard to keep up working relationships with more than just a few players at a time. Eventually, however, we got around to visiting Elmer.

Photo courtesy of Steve Marvill

Elmer Shaffer

Elmer is a middle-aged mechanic. He has played the guitar and mandolin ever since he was a young man. He always wanted to play the fiddle, but could never afford one. About fifteen years go, when Elmer was running his own television repair business, he fixed the set of a man who could not afford the bill. For his services, Elmer agreed to accept an old fiddle that his customer had stored away in his attic. With his knowledge of the mandolin, Elmer had a headstart when he began learning to fiddle.

Elmer's style is similar to Harry's. He is a dance fiddler. While not especially practiced at it, he also enjoys playing bluegrass. After winning third place in the first Central Pennsylvania Festival of the Arts fiddle contest, Elmer spent the rest of the afternoon and most of the evening jamming with other musicians, playing both bluegrass and oldtime.

Elmer has always been friendly and cooperative. He gladly shares his time with anyone interested in fiddling. Not long ago we invited Elmer and David Bell to State College to help us do a television show to promote our second fiddling contest. Elmer and David needed no prodding; they were pleased to be able to help out in any way they could. We were thankful that they would drive all the way to State College, taking a day off from work, to appear on a television show they knew little about. They trusted that we would not be frivolous with their time.

Bob and I have become more than just fiddle enthusiasts in our relationships with our players. Before we could work harmoniously with our fiddlers, we felt it was essential that we build a friendship with them. We wanted to interact, not just interview. This, I think, is a very important distinction. One can gain more than just field recordings if there is an exchange. A shared enjoyment of the time offers rewards mere interviewing misses.

In developing rapport, my original intention of learning to fiddle from our fiddlers played a very important role. We had, in their eyes, a practical need for the knowledge we sought. In addition, we were able to communicate on a common ground because we, like they, were musicians. In analyzing tunes and techniques, I also think it was essential that we had an intuitive understanding of what we were looking for. It is much easier for a musician to understand musicological phenomena than it is for a nonmusician. As musicians, we confronted the same learning and playing problems as the fiddlers and therefore are not inclined to offer "half-baked" explanations of seemingly unusual playing characteristics. Some of our players occasionally played pieces with irregular timing, but there was no consistency to the irregularities. When I found that they had not played some of the tunes in which they occurred for many years, I needed no further explanation for them. When an irregularity was repeated in a piece the player knew well, then I had cause to consider a musicological explanation.

It was invaluable for me to have played for square dances in order to understand why Harry plays the way he does. The problems confronting the dance fiddler help shape his style and techniques. The interaction between caller and fiddler can appear to be of little importance unless one has himself been confronted with the intricacy of the task.

Playing in a bluegrass band in many ways prepared me for studying the role of the fiddle in bluegrass. The implications of playing for an audience rather than a dance goes a long way toward explaining why bluegrass is different from traditional styles of playing. Taking only occasional solos rather than playing the lead nonstop is one aspect of bluegrass playing that colors the fiddler's approach. Another is that bluegrass players must be able to play in keys like B, B flat, and E. I might never have paid much attention to the techniques used for playing in these keys had I not needed to use them. After David showed me how he played in B, I practiced until I could do it. Then I began to watch other players to see if they used a similar technique. When I found that they did, only then did I make any generalizations.

The transmission and learning processes are very complex in any art, especially in an art for which there is no prescribed learning methodology. Having gone through the learning process myself, I noticed that other players experienced many of the same problems as I had. I felt obliged to point out and comment upon the ones I felt were fundamental to fiddling as a folk art.

I sincerely hope that any mistakes I might have made in transcribing or analyzing do not detract from my purpose. Some of my conclusions may be based on too few examples or may be too hastily drawn, but I believe further research will bear them out. I did seek advice and help in transcribing some of the more difficult passages. As far as variants are concerned, I omitted from the transcriptions many that were clearly just mistakes. I feel that the musical transcriptions, though they do omit certain variants and though I was ill-prepared to record misnotings, intentional or not, accurately relay and capture the tune versions and styles of our fiddlers.

Academically, I offer my research not as a final say but as a first say. I hope my efforts will be of value to folk music researchers by perhaps providing a starting point for more detailed study. To the more casual reader, I hope I have given an introduction to one of America's most widespread folk arts.

Returning to our collecting approach, I believe that nothing can surpass wanting to learn from someone when it comes to building a relationship with that person. Most of our players enjoyed teaching as much as I enjoyed learning. Playing was so much fun, however, that it was often difficult to stop in order to delve more deeply into areas which especially concerned us. The players themselves, though, rarely resisted specific questioning.

Photo courtesy of Dave Hamilton

Photo courtesy of Celia Wyckoff

Folklorists are sometimes concerned about too much exchange between collectors and informants. They fear regional or folkloric integrity might be polluted. I was aware that my habits and tunes might be picked up by fiddlers who had begun to learn from me. In all honesty, this did not overly concern me nor did it turn out to be much of a problem. I was careful never to prefer one tune or technique over another and I never drew attention to my own playing. In almost all situations the knowledge flowed in only one direction. The fiddlers, usually much older than I, appreciated my interest in their playing. They enjoyed the deference I showed toward both their age and their abilities.

Once, however, I played "Billy in the Low Ground" for David Bell and he liked the piece so much that he wanted me to teach it to him. Not only did I show him how to play it, I even recorded it on a cassette so that he could learn it at his leisure. I do not think that his having learned a tune from me in any way infringed upon the folkloric integrity of his style or repertoire.

Any collection project must have give and take from all parties. Had we nothing to return, I feel Bob and I would never have received what we did from our fiddlers. Moreover, topics and ideas simply would not have arisen in strictly question and answer periods. It is practically impossible to remember to ask everything during a formal interview. If one is trying to record all a fiddler's tunes, it is a great help to be able to spark his memory. The only way to do that is to play or hum bits of certain pieces, to see if he knows them. Many times a fiddler will not remember a tune by name and must be reminded how it goes musically.

There is something very rewarding about having sought out the friendship and knowledge of someone who by age, occupation, or lack of proximity might otherwise be totally beyond one's realm of acquaintances. I cannot stress strongly enough how important it was for Bob and me to have reached beyond our immediate purpose toward a full interaction with our players. To work with people who enjoy working with you is a rewarding and profitable experience. Such an experience lives on beyond the conclusion of the formal aspects of any project. With some of our fiddlers, our "project" will never end.

Bob and I met people whose friendship we cherish and from whom we gained knowledge which would never have otherwise been within our reach. With there being so many more fine folk musicians, we would be foolish to abandon our collecting project. Already Bob and I know at least a half dozen fiddlers within a reasonable distance whom we plan to seek out and record. All we need is more time.

Glossary of Terms

Aeolian: A mode or musical scale composed of eight tones, if we include the doubling of the tonic at the octave, which differs from the Ionian or major mode in that half steps lie between the second and third and between the fifth and sixth intervals. All other intervals between consecutive tones are one whole step. Playing A to A on the white keys of a piano yields an Aeolian scale.

Barring: A technique used by players of fretted instruments whereby the index finger holds down all the strings at one fret simultaneously.

Call: Directions of the square dance caller. Each dance has specific directions which are dictated by the caller.

Capo: A mechanical device used by guitar and banjo players which in effect shortens the neck of the instrument. A capo holds down all the strings at a given fret, allowing the instrument to be played in different keys while using open position fingerings.

Chinrest: The wooden cup at the bottom of the fiddle on which the player rests his or her chin, or actually jaw.

Chord: The simultaneous playing of two or more tones.

Chunk: Musicians' slang for the sound made when the mandolin is strummed continually in syncopation with the beat.

Clawhammer: The oldtime style of banjo playing whereby the melody is played with a downstroke of the index finger. The other fingers follow with a brushing action over the rest of the strings. A droned fifth string is then played by the thumb.

Clog: A traditional dance of Scots-Irish origin and its musical accompaniment. Its rhythm is characteristically composed of repeating patterns of sixteenth and dotted eighth notes or of dotted eighth and sixteenth notes.

Dobro: A brand name which has become synonymous with a type of guitar. The strings are run over a metal resonator, somewhat like an inverted pie plate, which is set into the body of the guitar. The strings are tuned to an open chord and are not fretted but stopped with a metal slide similar to that used by steel guitar players.

Dorian: A mode or musical scale composed of eight tones, if we include the doubling of the tonic at the octave, which differs from the Ionian or major mode in that half steps lie between the second and third, and sixth and seventh intervals. All other intervals between consecutive tones are one whole step. Playing D to D on the white keys of a piano yields a Dorian scale.

Double stop: Fingering and bowing two strings at the same time.

Drone: A tone which is sounded continuously while other notes are being played. Fingering one string and at the same time playing the open adjacent string creates a drone. Droning is common in English, Scottish, and Irish folk music, the predecessors to American fiddling. The drone of the bagpipe is perhaps most exemplary. While providing a practical solution to the need for volume, droning satisfies an aesthetic tendency as well.

F hole: The holes in the top of the fiddle through which the resonant sound escapes.

Fourth: The fourth note of a diatonic scale or the interval which includes four tones of a diatonic scale. The first note of the scale is the first, the second is the second, the third is the third, the fourth is the fourth, etc. The intervals are likewise named according to the number of tones they embrace.

Frailing: See Clawhammer for definition. For a thorough discussion of frailing, see Pete Seeger, *How to Play the Five-String Banjo* (Beacon, N.Y.: published by the Author, 1962). The musical effect is ''boom-ditty-boom-ditty-boom.'' Finger-picking styles, both two and three finger, did exist before the 1930s but bear little or no resemblance to the Scruggs style, which has become integrally related to bluegrass.

Frog: The piece of wood at the bottom of the bow which both holds the hair and permits it to be tightened by way of a screw mechanism.

Hex: Slang in the Buffalo Valley for witch. The verb form means to bewitch.

Hoedown: A square dance.

Hornpipe: Both a dance, now more or less extinct in the United States, and the tune which usually accompanies the dance. Hornpipe tunes are still played in the United States but they are played like reels.

Ionian: The mode most commonly referred to as the major mode. Its half steps fall between the third and fourth, and seventh and eighth intervals of the scale. All other consecutive tones are a whole step apart. Playing C to C on the white keys of a piano yields an Ionian scale.

Jam: Musicians' slang for an informal playing session.

Jig: A dance or tune that originally accompanied the dance. Jig tunes may be played for square dances. A jig tune is usually in $^6/_8$ time; it can be in $^9/_8$ time, but rarely is in the United States. There are jigs, usually referred to as straight jigs, which were performed on the black minstrel stage and were in $^2/_4$ or $^4/_4$ time. Their rhythm was similar to that of a clog. $^6/_8$ tunes are also called quadrilles or cotillions by players in other parts of the country.

Lick: A player's term for a rhythmic or melodic ornament used to embellish a tune.

Major, Minor: An interval, such as a major or minor third, the first being two whole steps, the second being one and a half steps. Major and minor may also refer to chords or scales. A major chord or triad is composed of the tonic, the tone a major third above the tonic, and the tone a minor third above the major third or a fifth above the tonic. A minor chord or triad is composed of the tonic, the tone a minor third above the tonic, and the tone a major third above the minor third or a fifth above the tonic. A major scale is simply an Ionian scale. A minor scale has as its chief characteristic the minor third interval. Various minor scales may also differ from the major scale in that the sixth and/or seventh interval may be flatted and hence minor as well. The Aeolian mode, with its flatted third, sixth, and seventh, is the "natural" minor scale.

Mixolydian: A scale or mode different from the Ionian by its flatted seventh degree. Half steps lie between the third and fourth, and sixth and seventh intervals. All other consecutive intervals are one whole step apart. Playing G to G on the white keys of a piano yields a Mixolydian scale.

Mode: A musical scale.

Neutral tone: A scale tone which in playing is slightly augmented or diminished, but not to the extent that would necessitate its being marked sharp or flat. In minor tonalities the neutral tone most likely to occur is the slightly raised third. In major tonalities the most likely neutral tones are the slightly lowered third, seventh, and sometimes sixth, and the slightly raised fourth.

Pick-up notes: Notes not part of the first measure of a line which are used to introduce a melody or solo. Also known as anacruces.

Positions: There are seven hand positions or placements used to finger notes on the violin in classical playing. To simplify, the first position is the one where the hand is closest to the nut, and the seventh position is the one where the hand is closest to the end of the fingerboard. There is a certain overlap and interrelation of positions which has little to do with fiddling. Refer to violin instruction texts for a more detailed definition.

Pow-wow: A faith healing session.

Prime: The tonic. In a G major scale, G is the prime.

Promenade: A square dance call.

Reel: A dance or its accompanying music. Reel tunes, which are written in 2/4 or 4/4, are often played for square dances.

Round dance: Nonsquare dance dances: waltzes, schottisches, etc.

Rosin: The resin which is rubbed onto the bow hairs so that they grip and therefore vibrate the strings when drawn across them.

Set: A group of four couples assembled for square dancing.

Shuffling: Either a bowing pattern in which the bow is rocked back and forth between the strings in a patterned and repetitive way as exemplified by *(a),* or simply a rhythmic pattern executed on one, or more often two, strings. The second case can be exemplified by *(b),* which I have seen referred to as both the Nashville shuffle and the Georgia shuffle.

(a)

(b)

Sixth: The interval which includes six tones of a diatonic scale. There are both major and minor sixths. Sixth may refer to the sixth tone of a scale as well.

Tailpiece: The piece of wood at the bottom of the fiddle to which the strings are fastened.

Third: The interval which includes three tones of the diatonic scale. There are major and minor thirds. Third may also refer to the third tone of a scale.

Tonic: The fundamental or first tone from which a scale is derived or on which it is built.

Virginia reel: A contra dance popular at square dances.

48217

787.1
G977l

Gunthարp, Matthew G
Learning the fiddler's ways /
Matthew G. Guntharp ; foreword by
Samuel P. Bayard ; introd. by Robert
C. Doyle. -- University Park :
Pennsylvania State University
Press, c1980.
159 p. : ill. ; 21 cm. --
(Keystone books)

ISBN 0-271-00237-9

1. Fiddle tunes--History and
criticism. I. Title.
ML3561.F5G8 787'.1'0714
79-65825
MARC
MN

Library of Congress
00449 *05921192 803262 0313